Murder in Connecticut

Murder in Connecticut

The Shocking Crime That Destroyed
a Family and United a Community

MICHAEL BENSON

THE LYONS PRESS
Guilford, Connecticut

An imprint of The Globe Pequot Press

The Lyons Press is an imprint of The Globe Pequot Press.

Designed by Sheryl P. Kober

Library of Congress Cataloging-in-Publication Data

Benson, Michael.
  Murder in Connecticut : the shocking crime that destroyed a family
and united a community / Michael Benson.
      p. cm.
  Includes bibliographical references.
  ISBN 978-1-59921-495-5
  1. Murder–Connecticut–Cheshire–Case studies. 2. Murder–Investigation–Connecticut–Cheshire–Case studies. I. Title.
  HV6534.C394B45 2008
  364.152'3097467–dc22

                                                2008024505

Printed in the United States of America

10 9 8 7 6 5 4 3 2 1

This book is dedicated to the people of Cheshire, Connecticut, and its surrounding towns who refused to "die a little" when unspeakable evil invaded in the middle of the night. Their story is one that should be mandatory reading for grief counselors, all who grieve, and every community that has had the misfortune of suffering the cruelest of tragedies.

Contents

Preface: *Central Connecticut—A Lesson in*
How to Heal . . . . **ix**

Acknowledgments . . . . **xi**

Introduction: *Double-Locked Doors and Restless Nights* . . **xii**

1. *Outside the Stop & Shop* **1**

2. *The Waking Nightmare* **9**

3. *Immediate Aftermath.* **24**

4. *"I Sure Am Glad That I Didn't Run into Him".* **43**

5. *Komisarjevsky and Hayes* **49**

6. *"We Plan to Seek the Death Penalty".* **82**

7. *Services—Private and Public.* **91**

8. *Candlelight Vigil* **107**

9. *More Search Warrants.* **113**

10. *Angry Voices.* **117**

11. *"I Came Here to See What Evil Looked Like"* **125**

12. *Bartlem Park Rally and the Three-Strikes Controversy.* **134**

13. *A New Cohesion in Deaconwood* **140**

14. *The Congregation's Dilemma* **143**

15. *Autumn.* **149**

16. *Dr. Petit Writes a Letter* **160**

17. *The Cheshire Lights.* **169**

18. *Then It Happened Again.* **175**

19. *More Legislative Debate.* **177**

20. *March Madness: A Turning Point in the*
Healing Process **184**

21. *The Grieving Schools: Miss Porter's, Chase Collegiate,*
and Cheshire Academy **189**

22. *Forever Michaela* **199**

Contents

Afterword: *The Darkness and the Light*. 203

Appendix A: *911 Transcript* 204

Appendix B: *Cheshire Police Dispatch Log,*
   July 23, 2007. 218

Appendix C: *Glossary of People Mentioned* 222

Appendix D: Bibliography. 230

Appendix E: Where to Send Donations 236

Index 238

About the Author 242

Preface

Central Connecticut—A Lesson in How to Heal

During summer vacation, when I was nine years old growing up in a small town south of Rochester, New York, my next-door neighbor, a fourteen-year-old girl, and her sixteen-year-old friend from down the road went missing. They'd gone swimming in the creek by a railroad trestle early on a Saturday evening and had not returned. Their bodies were found a month later alongside the railroad tracks not far from my house.

The day after the bodies were found, Monroe County Sheriff Skinner told the local paper, "It looks like our man is a sex fiend. [The knife wounds] make it certain that this is a sex murder. . . . This is the most brutal case I've seen in this county in my thirty-seven years in the department."

The wounds were said to be a combination of stab wounds and "slashes." As a kid I had no way to process information like that, but it nonetheless made for a troubled sleep. The boogeyman was real, and he was nearby.

The murderer was never caught.

The neighborhood, once happy and a little bit loud, went silent. No one ever mentioned the murders. Doors were locked and kids were kept closer to home. The back fields, once crossed with dirt paths worn by the bare feet of playing children, now grew over, forever hidden by unchecked foliage.

No one discussed the thing that had happened. Within six months, it was as if those girls had never existed. In a sense my neighborhood died a little with the two victims.

I compare that dreary response to the inspiring celebration of human character that has blossomed in central Connecticut since three members of the Petit family were murdered during a home invasion on July 23, 2007, and I am filled with amazement and admiration. Although the fear and grief suffered by the survivors was the same as that which my community felt when I was a child, the way people dealt with their pain could not have been more different.

Instead of retreating, they marched forward. Rallying around the heroic words of the surviving husband and father, vigils were held in honor of the victims at first, then rallies in support of tougher legislation, then fund-raisers in support of the victims' favorite charities. The townspeople heard the call to action and they responded.

Acknowledgments

The author would like to thank the following individuals and organizations, without whose help the writing of this book would have been impossible: Megan Alexander, Anne Darrigan, my brilliant editor Meredith Davis, my agent Jake Elwell, Mrs. A. Burch Tracy Ford, Joe Fantasia, Scott Frommer, Justin Ivey, Brent Lane, Norm Mesel, Jessica Norton, Dayna and Elizabeth Ollero, Lisa Riera, Andrew and Christine Wyzga, Joe Williams, Chionn Wolfe, Linda Friedner Cowen, Shining Peace Upon the Petits, Survivors of Homicide, and all of the reporters who got there before me. For a complete listing of my sources, see the bibliography at the back of the book.

Introduction:

Double-Locked Doors and Restless Nights

In this cold, cold world, with its explosion of electronic media and information overload, the omnipresent grappling for our attention has led to entertainment forms that appeal solely to our baser instincts. Who—say, in 1950—could have predicted that there would be in the first years of the twenty-first century a briefly popular genre of film known as "torture porn?" Even in the mainstream—and by this I mean what used to be referred to as broadcast television—much of our entertainment is derived from the sophisticated simulation of violent death. In fiction we have all become amateur crime-scene investigators. In nonfiction we have granted a certain celebrity of infamy to those who commit the most shocking of crimes. Many true-crime books published these days change names to protect the innocent yet put the correct names of the criminals in bold letters right on the cover. There is an argument that it should be the other way around. Perhaps we should deny the sadistic and the sociopathic their fifteen minutes of fame, change their names when we write about them, put black bars across their eyes when we publish their photographs. It's a thought.

The best way to get from here—the world in which you can go into candy stores and buy Serial Killer Trading Cards—to there, a world in which criminals are routinely denied recognition, is to take baby steps. First step: Let's recognize the murderers whose deeds are briefly depicted in this book for what they are, pieces of slime whose crimes are so brutal and ugly and horrible that they could have lowered the quality of life for everyone, especially for those in the vicinity. Theirs was a crime against humanity that seeps into your pores and crawls into your dreams, that makes for double-locked doors and restless nights hearing phantom footsteps in the den below.

This is not the story of the two nonentities who attacked one summer night, although out of necessity they must appear. It is rather the story of an idyllic little town in central Connecticut—the town of Cheshire, population 29,000, median household income $80,466—a town that could have buckled under, its world sullied forever, a black spot evermore blocking it's sun, but instead did not.

It is the story of a community that has stuck together and supported one another during the hardest possible times—a community that, only in crisis, has discovered its own formidable strength.

It is a story of anger and how even the most liberal of neighbors have rethought their opinions of capital punishment.

And it is the story of a husband and father who lost everything yet somehow clung to his sanity, who in a town of thousands of lights became the brightest beacon of all.

This is a true story. When possible, the spoken word has been quoted verbatim. However, when that is not possible, conversations have been reconstructed as closely as possible to reality based on the recollections of those who spoke and those who heard those words. In places, there has been slight editing of spoken words, but only to improve readability. The denotations and connotations of the words remain unaltered. When requested, the anonymity of some sources has been protected.

Chapter 1:

Outside the Stop & Shop

A mind without conscience or shame is a predatory thing. If we could tap into the stream of consciousness of a sociopathic B&E man, we probably wouldn't recognize much—just a dark, dark place, a yearning for kicks, a need for that jazz that accompanies invading the sanctuary of others. With an exaggerated sense of self-domain, he is a creepy-crawl junkie. B&E men who work in the daytime spike their veins by breaking the boundaries, by being where they shouldn't be, by stealing others' belongings and making them their own. But there's a special breed of B&E man, the kind that works at night. For him there is an additional mainline adrenaline rush that comes from the risk—the risk that, while he creepy-crawls, he will wake an occupant. Maybe a man, but even better a wife in a nightgown, or better yet, a tiny feminine voice, frightened in the dark. And then there will be a situation that needs controlling...

Sunday evening, July 22, 2007. The two breaking and entering (B&E) men were trolling for victims—for someone with a house worth violating that night. Since one of them was a local, he knew the perfect spot. On the west side of the town's main drag, Highland Avenue, was the Maplecroft Shopping Plaza.

There was a Dress Barn, Marshalls department store, Rite Aid Pharmacy, Family Haircut, Hallmark, Subway, Cheshire Video, Jenny K Cleaners, and a Bank of America. The biggest and busiest store, however, was the grocery store called the Super Stop & Shop. They could sit for as long as they wanted and watch customers come and go. No one would say "boo."

Though most of the plaza was parallel to the road, the Super Stop & Shop, at the north end, ran perpendicular to the line of stores and the road. It was one of those gigantic megastores, a food planet, with aisles just for ketchup or for gluten-free foods. It had a People's United Bank and a Dunkin' Donuts built into it. There were entrances and exits on either end of the store. It would have been awkward to park and watch both, so the men picked one exit and parked facing it.

It had been a hot summer day, and even with the sun lowering in the sky, the temperature was still in the eighties. An attractive middle-aged mother and her eleven-year-old daughter, both blondes in shorts, exited the store carrying grocery bags. The men in the car sat up a little bit straighter.

The blondes radiated wholesome American perfection. It was as if the summer sun focused just on them—and the predators knew what that meant: affluence. The two had found what they were looking for.

The mother was Jennifer Hawke-Petit. Absolutely beautiful, but without a shred of vanity. She had spent her entire life nurturing others. As a mother and a school nurse at the town's boarding school, she spent all of her hours caring for others, a glowing surrogate mom to the community. As the pair climbed into the car, there was no indication that the mother had, for the past eight years, bravely battled multiple sclerosis, a disease of the central nervous system. The girl was her beautiful eleven-year-old daughter Michaela (pronounced Mi-KAY-la). They were part of the Petit family, which also included seventeen-year-old Hayley, and father Bill, a well-known doctor.

Maybe the younger of the two men recognized the mother and daughter. He was a "townie." When he wasn't in jail, he was usually nearby. And the Petits were well-known around town.

Many people who didn't know them personally knew who they were. They were social leaders. There was a solid chance he'd seen them around.

As Jennifer drove the white Mercedes out of the parking lot and onto Route 10, she and her daughter were less than ten minutes from home and only a couple of hundred yards from where Jennifer worked. Feeling safe and happy, they were completely unaware that a pair of monsters was on their tail.

The two men shadowed the white Mercedes from a safe distance as the mother and daughter drove the serpentine route to their home on the west side of town, in the Deaconwood neighborhood of Cheshire. The white car pulled into the driveway of a luxurious home on hilly Sorghum Mill Drive, three miles from the Super Stop & Shop. It was a beige clapboard colonial on a corner lot. The men following them didn't need the real estate stats to figure it out: The family was wealthy.

Although the house's address was 300 Sorghum Mill Drive, the house faced Hotchkiss Ridge. Only the garage built onto the side of the house faced Sorghum Mill Drive. The house must have been worth a half-million dollars. The house was set back from the street and, especially from the garage side, partially obscured by trees.

Money and blondes. The monsters felt that they had found the perfect target. And make no mistake, they needed money. One needed his daily fix of pot and crack cocaine. The other was hooked on methamphetamine.

The stalkers didn't stop. They made a mental note of the address and kept driving. They'd be back. There were preparations to be made. They drove to the Wal-Mart in the nearby town of Wallingford, where they bought an air rifle and rope. If someone woke up, the men would need a way to handle it.

The air rifle was to subdue; the rope was to restrain. Their shopping done, they each went home for a few hours.

The younger one called his ex-girlfriend. No, make that girlfriend. Her father had taken her south to Arkansas. All he needed, he told her, was money to bring her back. She wasn't sure what he meant by that, but that was what he said. Lots of money, he said. Fifteen large. He told her he'd get it. Soon. The girlfriend would later recall that he seemed "jumpy," like he wanted "to get somewhere and do something."

At close to midnight, the men left their homes and met up once again. On his way out, the young one had to listen to his mom yak. Why was he going out so late? Why was he wearing dark clothes? He told her he was meeting a guy named Steve about a job.

They started out in two vehicles and drove back to the Maplecroft Plaza, parked one, and drove together in the other. Then they went to the mother and daughter's neighborhood and found a secluded site down the street. There they parked. And waited.

What an odd pair to be in Cheshire, Connecticut, a town that looked like a postcard picture. Cheshire was straight out of a 1950s movie about life in Everytown, USA.

As you came into town, the sign said:

WELCOME TO CHESHIRE
The Bedding Plant Capital of Connecticut

Cheshire, Connecticut, is in the geographic center of the state. At the time of the crime, it had a population of 29,000 and a land area of 32.9 square miles. Like the rest of central

Connecticut, the land was undulating and the roads were winding. If you were waiting for a flat stretch of straight road to pass the truck in front of you, you'd have a long wait. Every road had solid double lines down the center. It was a town where houses tended to be set back from the road, often with trees between the houses and the street. Good for hiding. Hiding and watching.

The town had forty-five police officers and six detectives. It was once a market town for farmers, and there were still plenty of farmers on the outskirts growing flowers and vegetables for sale locally and in other areas. By the twenty-first century it also functioned as a suburb of Hartford and New Haven, and many residents were business people and professionals who worked in the city.

The hills were not just woodsy, they were rocky as well. Great boulders and ledges stuck out—as if the great glacier of the Ice Age had been particularly aggressive when slouching its way through Cheshire. It was a town where there were still houses more than two hundred years old, and yet there was new construction everywhere. For years now the open fields had been disappearing, replaced by housing.

All of the houses were well kept and different from one another. Families had dogs. No one lived too far from Main Street. And even here, in this pleasantest of towns, the thirty-year-old house and its sylvan surroundings on the corner of Sorghum Mill Drive and Hotchkiss Ridge seemed special. And, as many townsfolk knew, the residents of that house were special as well.

Inside the house was domestic bliss. Though there were often guests—people loved to go there because of the warmth, the hospitality, and the fun—today it was just family. Dad was

5

home. Being a physician, he had little spare time, but it was Sunday and he'd managed to get in eighteen holes of golf with *his* dad. He was Dr. William A. Petit Jr., one of the world's leading authorities on the treatment of diabetes.

The house had eight rooms, a sun porch, and a brick fireplace. In the backyard there was a basketball hoop and an enclosed trampoline. In the garage there were crates filled with soccer balls and lacrosse sticks. Dr. Petit, Jennifer, Hayley, (known as Haze to family and friends) and Michaela, (nicknamed KayKay) were all home. The whole family was together on a Sunday.

They were an active family. If there was a cause worth working for, chances were they were on the front lines. If money needed to be raised or a neighbor needed help, they were there, no questions asked. The charitable cause that took most of their time was multiple sclerosis, which made sense. That was the ugly disease that had attacked their family.

Earlier in the day the two daughters had found time to go to the beach club for a swim. Now it was Michaela's turn to make dinner. That had been the reason to go to the Super Stop & Shop. They needed to get the ingredients for one of Michaela's vegetarian masterpieces.

If Michaela was watching TV, chances were good that the budding young chef was watching the Food Network, trying to pick up some tips. On this night, she made a pasta sauce of native tomatoes, garlic, olive oil, and basil, and she mixed up a balsamic vinaigrette for the salad. Her dream was to one day concoct, like a mad scientist, the perfect root-beer float.

Daughter Hayley was the jock of the family. She rowed on her high-school crew team and had been a basketball star. She was also co-editor of her high school's literary magazine. Usually healthy, she'd had her problems recently, too, having been briefly hospitalized just before graduation with a collapsed lung.

"She had to make it to that graduation ceremony. She was not going to let her class down," her high-school principal Mrs. Ford later recalled.

Hayley had plans, too. She was going to be a doctor like her father. Medicine had been her career ambition ever since her father gave her a child-size medical bag and instruments for her fourth birthday. Her all-time favorite TV show was *Dr. Quinn, Medicine Woman*. It was her idea to name her kid sister Michaela in honor of that show's main character, Michaela Quinn.

She had been accepted at Dartmouth. Early admission. Dad's alma mater. Just a month before, the house had been the scene of a joyous party, celebrating Hayley's graduation from the all-girls Miss Porter's School in Farmington. Tables were set up outside. In the center of each table was a bouquet of daisies. Daisies have great symbolic meaning to students at Miss Porter's School, who often refer to themselves by the unofficial nickname the Fighting Daisies. A student gathering place at the school is known as the Daisy Café. Daisies are a strong and robust flower that can thrive under all sorts of circumstances. They are bright and beautiful, yet they endure, and are useful in a wide variety of ways. Because of this, daisies have been part of girls' school tradition since the nineteenth century. In a lovely, final ritual, each graduation at Miss Porter's featured a thick woven chain of daisies that was carried by all the students as they sang. And then a portion of the chain was taken and placed on the grave of Sarah Porter, the school's founder, who was buried not far from the school.

Everyone knew that Hayley was smart and athletic and really into school. But her friends knew she also had a sly sense of humor. She knew how to have a good time. She knew how to make you laugh and smile.

Dr. and Mrs. Petit couldn't have been more proud of the lovely way their children had turned out.

The pasta dinner was delicious. Afterward the girls read *Harry Potter*. Hayley was reading the last book in the series. Michaela was reading the first.

It grew dark.

Chapter 2:

The Waking Nightmare

Two burglars were wearing hooded sweatshirts as they entered the Petit home through the basement door at 3:00 a.m. It was July 23, 2007. The night air was cooler, about 65 degrees. And damp—felt like a storm might be coming. They weren't surprised to find the door unlocked. Cheshire was the kind of town where some people even left their front doors open at night. They felt so safe that they didn't see the need to lock them.

The two men had assumed that everyone would be upstairs asleep, as was almost always the case when they entered homes in the middle of the night.

And they had been entering homes in the middle of the night frequently. This was at least the third house they had illegally entered that weekend. They had gotten into the first two through back screen doors, but hadn't netted much: $140 in cash, credit cards, and an ATM card. This night would be different. This was the mother lode.

This burglary was different in another way, too. On the sun porch, asleep in an easy chair, was Dr. Petit. The intrusion either woke him, or the intruders feared he would wake. Either way, the two men knew they had two choices: run or attack.

They attacked, hitting the man in the forehead with a baseball bat. Now unconscious, Dr. Petit was tied up at the hands and ankles, and then pushed down the cellar stairs. With the husband out of commission, the mother and her two daughters were alone with the monsters. Defenseless.

At approximately 4:30 a.m., about an hour and a half into the attack, the two men exited the Petit home together, leaving their captives bound and helpless. Something must've happened. Maybe one of their captives recognized them. Maybe they just felt overcome by a mean streak. Whatever it was, they had decided how this show was going to end.

The young man drove his own car. The older man stole one of the Petits' vehicles, probably the SUV. They drove to the intersection of Prospect Road and West Main Street, where they filled plastic containers with gasoline at a BP gas station.

The BP was perfect because there were slots right on the gas pumps, so they could put their stolen credit card in and it automatically charged the card for the gas. They didn't have to deal with any real live human being who might wonder why they wanted so much gas in containers during the middle of the night.

They put the full containers in the Petits' car.

Directly across the street from the gas station was the rocky side of a hill that had been blasted out so the road could go through. Diagonally across, about fifty yards east of the gas station, was the entrance to a housing development called Quarry Village. On either side of the entrance were two stone pedestals with old-fashioned street lamps on top. Outside of those were wooden gates, painted bright white. The young man drove his car into the Quarry Village complex, past the sign that said, "No Soliciting. Private Property. Violators Will Be Prosecuted."

The houses were multilevel, but more out of necessity than design, because the entire development was on a hill. A garage might be at the bottom of the hill, while the front door was at the top. Each house was painted the same shade of industrial gray with white trim.

The speed limit on Quarry Village Road was twenty miles per hour, and a sign read, "Slow. Children Playing." The younger man parked in a small parking lot—big enough for eight to ten cars at most—at the side of the entrance road. He climbed into the Petit vehicle with the older man. They then returned to the Maplecroft Plaza parking lot, dropped off a few items in their other vehicle, and returned to the Petit house. The outing probably took about twenty minutes, certainly less than half an hour.

As the early summer morning lightened the sky, the intruders had concocted a scheme that would net big bucks. They told the mother that, if she wanted to save the lives of her daughters, she would go with one of them to the bank, withdraw $15,000, and return. Do as they said, and everything would be okay. If not, well, things would go badly.

And so, in a desperate attempt to keep her daughters alive, Jennifer agreed to go to the bank as soon as it opened in the morning with one of the invaders. If only they would leave. "Deal," the men said, but reminded her that if anyone called the cops, her husband and daughters were dead. She said she understood. At 9:00 a.m. the older man took Jennifer out to her car. The young man remained behind to take care of some things at the Petit home.

At 9:19 a.m. the older man arrived with the mother at the Bank of America branch on Highland Avenue in Cheshire. It was only a few hundred yards from where the men had first spotted Jennifer and Michaela the previous day, at the opposite end of the shopping plaza.

It was an overcast Monday morning. Inside the bank, everyone was moving slowly, holding cardboard containers of coffee and softly discussing weekend activities. Jennifer entered the front door through the vestibule that held the ATM machine. She had to take a left to get into the main part of the bank that housed the tellers and customer service. Straight ahead was a large glass window to the manager's office, but you couldn't see in because the blinds were down and closed.

The bank had just opened and there was already a pretty good crowd. Everyone liked to get their banking done first thing on Monday morning so they could get on with their week. There were about twenty people waiting in line for one of the five tellers, a couple of more using the ATM machines, and one woman sitting at a customer service desk talking to a bank employee about opening a new account.

The older man parked his car right in front of the bank, positioning himself so that he would be able to look inside and see what his hostage was doing. If it looked like she was squealing, he wanted to know right away so he'd have an opportunity to hightail it out of there.

He allowed Jennifer to go into the bank alone. They had agreed that she would withdraw $15,000 from her savings account, and then immediately return to the car. Her hands were shaking so badly that she had trouble writing on the withdrawal slip, but finally she managed it.

The already-long wait for an available teller was made worse by stress, and she finally decided to cut the line. Her face displayed so much urgency that no one complained. If she was trying to camouflage her predicament, she was not successful. Others in the bank could tell by the grim expression on Jennifer's face that something was wrong.

She went to the last teller, in the far corner of the bank. She pushed the small piece of paper through the slot at the base of the window. Banks were keen to pick up on suspicious activity, so even without Jennifer's nervous demeanor, withdrawing that much money in cash would have raised a red flag.

The teller looked at the piece of paper and saw that it was not a routine withdrawal slip but a message. Jennifer had written something to the effect of, "I need to take $15,000 out of my savings account in cash. I have to have the money because my family is being held hostage. If the police are notified my family will be killed."

One of the customers in the bank at that moment was fifty-year-old former graphic artist Deborah "Debbie" Biggins, who was opening a new checking account. She took note of Jennifer because the woman seemed unusually tense and in a rush.

"I was feeling impatient about getting the paperwork for my new account started. The next thing I knew, I looked over and saw a tall blonde woman. I saw she was holding a white piece of paper and I thought it was a deposit slip or a receipt," Biggins later recalled. She could feel the fear emanating from the woman. "She was stiff. It was all bad. I felt it."

After Jennifer left with the money, Biggins saw the teller hand Jennifer's note to the bank manager, who was a woman named Mary Lyons.

"I saw the teller hand the slip of paper to the manager, and the manager walked right behind me to her office. The manager then peeked through the blinds of her office, looking at something out in the parking lot, and a sense of panic fell on me. I thought the bank was being robbed. I asked the customer service rep, 'What's going on?'"

The customer service rep didn't know but was obviously just as concerned. Letting her finger slip from the window blinds, Mary Lyons reached for the phone.

Lyons called the police to report suspicious activity. According to police, that call was received at 9:21 a.m. She said that it appeared as if one of their customers was taking out cash under duress.

More than once Lyons was put on hold by the dispatch operator. She was then told to call back on another line with a further description of what had occurred at the bank.

It took approximately five minutes before the incident at the bank was first broadcast to police in the field at 9:26 a.m., including the name of the nervous woman who had withdrawn the money, and her home address, 300 Sorghum Mill Drive.

The older man had the blonde mother in the front seat with him where he could keep an eye on her. It seemed like it took forever to get out of the parking lot. A red light then held him up before he could pull onto Highland Avenue, heading south, past St. Peter's Episcopal Church, right past the Cheshire Academy where Jennifer worked, through the posh section of town, past the First Congregational Church, which had been built hundreds of years before but had been recently painted. It was shining white with four columns in front and a high steeple and clock tower. There was a small park between the church and the road.

They turned right and wound their way along Cornwall Avenue. The houses on either side of the road were large. Some had been built large. Others had been small once but had undergone several expansive renovations.

The world was up and at it. There may have been joggers running alongside the road, people walking their dogs, neighbors out by the mailbox talking about Sunday night's television shows.

They drove past the Farmington Linear Park Bike Route (commonly known to Cheshire residents as "the bike trail"), Cheshire Roofing, and a nail salon, then past farmhouses with lots of land and huge gardens, and Doolittle School's ball fields. There were a couple of stop signs, but who knows if the man stopped.

Up ahead was a tree-covered mountain, at the base of which was Mountain Road, where they turned left. They stayed on Mountain for only two blocks before making another left onto Sorghum Mill Drive, through a hundred yards of woods and a few more blocks of houses. The area was so hilly that even the front lawns had hills in them. It could be hard to figure out street addresses, but some houses had put their street numbers on rocks near the road.

The older of the two predators then pulled up and into the woman's driveway. The trip from the bank had taken approximately seven minutes.

Debbie Biggins was still in the bank when the police arrived. She recalled, "Not long afterward the police rushed in—at least five officers—and they fanned out through the lobby. They left right away without talking to any customers."

"What is happening?" Biggins asked a bank employee.

"It's just something that happened outside, it has nothing to do with us," the bank employee replied.

In the meantime, back at the police dispatch, there was some confusion. According to an anonymous law enforcement official, "The call [from Mary Lyons] came in as a suspicious transaction with a hostage situation, but it wasn't clear."

That first broadcast referred to an "incident" at the Petit house and gave a description of the car that had been used to take Mrs. Petit to and from the bank. The first officer who responded to the radio dispatch call to head to Sorghum Mill Drive was on Higgins Road just past Oak Avenue—less than a mile from the Petit home.

At 9:27, the officer at Higgins and Oak said, "What was that number on Sorghum?"

"Three hundred Sorghum Mill Road. Three-hundred," dispatch said.

"Unit one copy, I'm turning there now," the first-responding officer replied.

The cop made a quick K-turn on Higgins Road and headed west. He zoomed past Watch Hill Road on the right and Towpath Lane on the left before taking a right onto Sorghum Mill Drive. The street only went thirty yards or so before it curved sharply left, a sharp enough turn that even a police car would need to slow down. Then up a hill and past a wood on the right, he arrived outside the Petit home at 9:28. He was instructed not to approach the house. So he walked behind the house and hid behind a tree, watching the rear of the house.

After a few minutes other cops showed up as well. They saw that there was a 2005 Chrysler Pacifica SUV in the driveway, which belonged to the Petits. The other car in the driveway was the white Mercedes that the mother and daughter had used to make their Super Stop & Shop run the previous evening.

A computer check popped out the license plate numbers for both of the Petit vehicles, and sure enough, those were the only two vehicles in the Petit driveway.

Despite the five-minute gap between when Mary Lyons called 911 and when police dispatch first broadcast the "incident at 300 Sorghum Mill Drive" to police officers, it was still a seven-minute drive from the bank to the home, and later law enforcement officials would, under assurance of anonymity, wonder how the older man got to the house before the first police officer. But he did.

Minutes later, more police officers arrived at the scene, but no one knocked on the door. On the police radio a voice could be heard saying, "Hang back from that location."

Because the initial 911 call had said that the family would be killed if the cops came, none of the police officers were in a hurry to bust down the door and charge inside the house. They would wait, try not to be noticed, and act only when ordered to do so.

The orders came down to wait until there were sufficient numbers to raid the house. Members of the SWAT team were summoned, which was known as the SRT (Special Response Team) in Cheshire. Some police called in and asked for their tactical (that is, bulletproof) vests to be brought to them from headquarters where they had left them. The sky was not brightening. Dark clouds hung low. The Petit house was hard enough to see from the street under the brightest of conditions. It was even harder with a summer rainstorm about to strike.

At 9:44 police dispatch broadcast the phone number for the Petit home. No one called the number.

By 9:54 many law enforcement personnel, including SRT members, were on the scene, establishing a perimeter around the Petit house. (See appendices for a transcript of police activity for the thirty minutes following the Bank of America 911 call.) With everything in the house quiet, police waited.

And waited.

As soon as the older man and Jennifer had returned home from their trip to the bank, he strangled her to death and left her atop a coffee table on the first floor of her home. Hayley and Michaela were still bound to their beds with rope upstairs.

Down in the basement, his head still bleeding from the bat attack, Dr. Petit woke to what he believed to be the sound of his wife screaming. Even though he was suffering from a severe concussion and he felt as if his skull had been cracked open, he managed to free his hands.

His fingers were stiff and wouldn't work right. He tried and tried but couldn't undo his legs. So he did the next best thing. He began to hop. When he fell, he got back up and hopped some more. He hopped up the cellar stairs, crashed out the back door, and hopped into the backyard.

Unaware that the police were already surrounding his house, he had one thing on his mind—to incite his neighbors into calling the police. His desperate anguish could be heard by the police officers in the vicinity.

"We got an eighteen [Cheshire Police code for a person] somewhere out . . . it sounds like it's coming from your direction, so just be aware of it. Sounds like he's outside, somebody's outside anyhow," an officer said.

Unfortunately, Dr. Petit's cries could also be heard by the two men inside the Petit house. He got as far as the house next door at 285 Hotchkiss Ridge before collapsing from exhaustion and from the effects of his head wounds.

Still not approaching the Petit home, police went to William Petit's aid. The wounded man lay prone on the ground under his neighbor's overhang, the house directly to the east of the Petit home.

Police saw right away that the man was suffering from severe head injuries. Blood still oozed from a wound on his forehead above his right eyebrow. He had tumbled onto his right side and his ankles were bound together with interlocked plastic zip ties.

A neighbor heard Dr. Petit's shouting and made a second 911 call to the police. One of the home invaders peeked out an upstairs bedroom window. They knew that they had to act quickly.

The men poured gasoline around and on Jennifer's body and on Hayley and Michaela, who were still alive. The criminals thought they were smart. They thought they would get away clean if they could just incinerate the DNA they had so cruelly deposited at the scene.

They lit the fire and left the house. They ran out the front door of the house and climbed into the Petits' Pacifica.

Police radios squawked: "We got a house fire. We gotta clear the house."

It was 9:58 and it was starting to rain. Outside, police could hear horrible screams coming from the upstairs bedrooms.

The bleeding man under the overhang said he was William Petit, the homeowner of the house on fire, and that his wife and two daughters were still inside. He'd heard screaming. He begged the police to hurry. He told them that his family had been the victims of a home invasion, and that burglars had hit him on the head, tied him up, and shoved him into the basement of his house. An ambulance would arrive a few minutes later and take him to St. Mary's Hospital in Waterbury.

As police went to Dr. Petit's aid, other police stationed near the Petit driveway saw two panicky white men exit the house, hurriedly jump into the Petits' SUV, and back out of the driveway. The police shouted in vain for the men in the vehicle to stop. The SUV continued recklessly into the street, smashed into a cop car, and pulled away, heading north. The police cars in front of the Petit home turned on their lights and sirens.

The driver tried to make a getaway down the street, unaware that two Cheshire police cars, belonging to SRT team members Sergeant Chris Cote and Officer Tom Wright, were parked nose-to-nose blocking the street at the spot where Burrage Court made a T with Sorghum Mill Drive. Cote and Wright had left their cars and, carrying semiautomatic rifles, were headed for the Petit house. Stationed at the roadblock was Officer Jeff Sutherland.

When the driver saw Sutherland standing in the street and the two cop cars blocking his way, he gunned the engine and aimed the vehicle at Sutherland. The officer managed to get out of the way, but the SUV crashed into both cruisers. The front end of the SUV and those of both cop cars were smashed in by the impact. The police cars were struck so hard that they spun apart, opening up the street.

Fortunately for the police at the scene, the impact was also hard enough to disable the SUV and cause its front-seat air bags to deploy. The Pacifica rolled to a stop thirty feet further down Sorghum Mill Drive, which suddenly looked like the site of a demolition derby. The SUV's front tires rested on a neighbor's finely manicured lawn.

At that moment, a neighbor named Walter Ryan was walking his dog along Sorghum Mill Drive. "I saw the car come out of the driveway and ram into several police cars. Then I saw the flames coming out of the house. Then I saw police with their guns out, running across the lawns yelling, 'Get out of the car!'" Ryan said.

When police hauled the assailants out of the SUV, they could see that they were an odd couple. One of the men appeared to be in his twenties, the other middle-aged. The young man was tall and thin with thick hair. The older man was short and stocky, his head shaved bald.

The young man, who had been driving, was wearing DeWalt work boots, two pairs of white athletic socks, a pair of grey boxer-briefs, a pair of Carhartt pants, a long-sleeved black T-shirt, an Adidas hoodie, a pair of cotton work gloves, and a pair of light-colored latex gloves. He was subsequently identified as Joshua Komisarjevsky (Koh-mih-sahr-JEV-skee), born August 10, 1980, a career criminal with a long history of breaking-and-entering offenses.

The middle-aged man, who had been a passenger during the truncated escape attempt, was later identified as Steven J. Hayes, born May 30, 1963. He was wearing a blue hoodie, a gray cotton T-shirt, black socks, and Adidas sneakers.

Both were out of prison on parole.

Lying in the road next to the car was a cell phone. Police processed it as part of the crime scene, and later found it to be Komisarjevsky's cell.

As soon as the men were taken into custody they were transported to the Cheshire Police Department, located at 500 Highland Avenue.

As the apprehension took place, the house fire rapidly worsened. The Cheshire Fire Department was on its way. The rain was growing harder, steadier.

Police officers opened the home's front door and observed a "line of fire" consisting of a bright orange flame on the floor and in the hallway. There was no more screaming.

The fire department showed up and quickly put out the fire. It was 10:01 a.m., thirty-one minutes since the 911 call from the bank.

And it was then, with the attackers in custody and Dr. Petit on his way to the hospital, that the firemen inside the burning home discovered the full horror of the situation. There, they found three lifeless bodies.

As Dr. Petit's father, William Petit Sr., would later say, "Five minutes earlier, and they would have saved everyone—but that's not the way it worked."

Found inside the home and seized were three plastic, opaque, partially melted one-gallon containers. Two of these containers were found on the second-floor landing, while a third was found in the first-floor hallway.

State troopers were called in. Homicide detectives were notified. The county medical examiner was called. Sorghum Mill Drive was blocked off to traffic on both sides. The house and the cars were all crime scenes.

By noon a deluge was falling upon Cheshire, and it was making life even more miserable for the police, who were attempting to figure out what had happened at the Petit home. They put up a tent in the middle of the street so that they could stay relatively dry as they compared notes.

Crime-scene investigators processed the Petit family vehicle, the 2005 Chrysler Pacifica that had been stolen by the two men and crashed into the police cars blocking the street. They photographed and seized several items from the vehicle. These included a black Carhartt winter cap with what appeared to be eyeholes cut in it, five latex gloves, two white cotton gloves, and four separate sets of interlocking plastic zip ties.

Komisarjevsky's car, a 1998 Chevrolet Venture, was found a mile and a half from the scene of the murders, in the parking lot of the Quarry Village housing complex. Investigators determined that it had been utilized in the crimes. Just down the street from the complex was the gas station where the men had filled their plastic containers.

Crime-scene investigators processed the Venture and photographed and seized two empty packages of Stanley latex gloves, nine pairs of latex gloves (five white, three "light-colored," and one blue), two black-and-blue rubber gloves, an open package of GE eight-inch cable ties, and a brown cotton shirt that had two holes cut in the back portion of it, which were suspected to be eyeholes.

Police located and searched Hayes's vehicle, which was parked in the Super Stop & Shop parking lot. They photographed and seized two wallets from that vehicle. One contained identification for Hayley Petit, and the other contained the ID of William Petit. Sometime during the night one or both of the intruders had made a run out to Hayes's car and then returned to the Petit home, probably during the gasoline run.

Investigators learned that Steven Hayes lived in Winsted, about thirty miles away. Joshua Komisarjevsky, on the other hand, lived right in Cheshire, at 840 North Brooksvale Road, in a dilapidated old house that was 1.8 miles away from the crime scene. During the course of their investigation, police would thoroughly search the homes of both men, but before they could do that, they needed to consult a judge and obtain search warrants.

Investigators were running on instinct. They were so well trained that they made correct decisions and asked the right questions despite the fact that their brains were on fire with the horror of the morning. Still, they had to push on. If justice were to be served, they couldn't make any mistakes.

Chapter 3:

Immediate Aftermath

At noon, after informing Dr. Petit at the hospital that his family was gone, police realized that something was going to have to be done about the media. The town was abuzz with rumors only hours after the events of the morning had come to their violent conclusion. The Connecticut State Police decided to hold a press conference so that the members of the media who were entering the small town would all be on the same page.

The press conference, held at the 500 Highland Avenue headquarters of the Cheshire Police Department, was called to order by Lieutenant J. Paul Vance of the Connecticut State Police. Lieutenant Vance said:

This is a press conference called regarding events that took place this morning here in the town of Cheshire sometime around 9:30 this morning. First of all, I need to stress to you that this case is ongoing as we speak, and there are many areas we still are not able to discuss or give details on as we anticipate charges to be filed.

The facts are as follows: This morning shortly after 9:30 a suspicious incident took place at the Bank of America in the Maplecroft Plaza here in the town of Cheshire. The employees of the Bank of America thought the activities were suspicious enough that they contacted the Cheshire Police Department and advised them of the suspicious incident.

The Cheshire police dispatched officers to the vicinity of the bank and to the area of the victim's residence in an attempt and an effort to intercept the vehicle involved in

24

this suspicious behavior that took place at the bank. Several police officers responded to the area of the bank as well as to the area of the victim's residence.

Upon arrival at the victim's residence, an officer observed two male subjects exit a private residence and also observed the private residence fully engulfed in flames. The first responding officer attempted to intercept the two suspects as they exited the driveway in a vehicle.

The suspect vehicle rammed the Cheshire police officer's car and continued on Sorghum Mill Road. While the suspect vehicle was fleeing from that first accident, two additional Cheshire police officers positioned their vehicles to intercept the suspect vehicle. Observing the Cheshire police officer's vehicles, the suspects increased their speed and rammed two additional Cheshire police cars. All of the police officers involved in these two incidents were not injured. At that point two officers from Cheshire PD were able to approach the suspects and were able to take them into custody without incident.

The Cheshire Fire Department responded to the fire scene, and upon suppression of the fire were able to enter the residence and discovered the remains of three victims.

Cheshire police officers were assigned to secure the residence, the bank, and the two accident sites as crime scenes.

Both of the individuals have been transported here to Cheshire Police Headquarters. They are in the process of being booked at this time. Cheshire Police Chief Michael Cruess requested the assistance of the Connecticut State Police Major Crime Squad and the Office of the State Fire Marshal to work with the Cheshire Police Department and the New Haven State Attorney's Office in this investigation.

It is important for me to mention again that this is a very extensive investigation. I know there are many details and many rumors out there that we will not be able to con-firm at this time.

Cheshire Police Chief Michael Cruess next spoke to the gathered media:

This is a very unfortunate, tragic incident that is probably going to reach right down to the core of the community.

I want to assure the residents of Cheshire that everybody is safe. This is an isolated incident. The two suspects, the people involved, were caught—caught right down the road, didn't even get a quarter of a mile away. The neighborhood is safe. The town is safe.

One male individual was able to exit the victims' home and has been transported to St. Mary's Hospital, where he is reported to be in serious but stable condition.

The identities of the deceased are not going to be released pending a postmortem examination by the state's medical examiner to determine the precise cause and manner of death—and to establish positive identification.

If any officers who had been part of that morning's activities were within earshot of the press conference, they would have noticed some interesting omissions. The claim that "the first-responding officer" noticed "upon arriving" that the house was on fire and men were trying to escape was plain wrong. Completely missing in the statement to the press was the five-minute gap between the first 911 call and the order to send police to the Petit house, as well as the more glaring twenty-six-minute gap between when officers first arrived in the vicinity of the Petit house and when they first took action.

As the press was apprised if not appeased, the Cheshire Police Department and the Connecticut State Police Central District Major Crime Squad had already undertaken a joint investigation to determine the facts and circumstances surrounding the deaths of Dr. Petit's family. The Petit home was given over to crime-scene investigators (CSIs) who went over the entire residence with a fine-tooth comb. Involved in the processing of the scene were Major Crime Squad investigators, along with the State Police Fire Marshal Unit. Anything of evidentiary value was located, documented, and seized.

During this process, investigators observed that Jennifer had remnants of a nylon-type material burnt in the area of the back of her neck and a charred ropelike material in the area of her ankles. Investigators also observed and photographed a ropelike material on the extremities of both Hayley and Michaela. They also found a ropelike material tied to the bedposts of both girls' beds. Both victims were found spread-eagle with all extremities tied to the bedposts, suggesting possible sexual assault.

Jennifer's body had been burned beyond recognition—and there was evidence that fire accelerant had been liberally poured directly onto her. The bodies of Hayley and Michaela also showed signs that accelerant had been poured directly onto them, or near them, but not to the same degree as their mother.

The fire marshals quickly came to the conclusion that arson was the cause of the fire. They discovered patterns consistent with an accelerant being poured in various locations throughout the residence, along with unusual burn patterns as a result of the accelerant pours.

Also leading to the conclusion of arson was the "line of fire" in the first-floor hallway that police had observed when they first entered the house, and the three one-gallon containers police had found inside the home.

Across the street from the Petit home, two teenaged siblings sat on the lawn and watched all of the police and fire department activity in amazement. They were Mark and Morgan Raducha, sixteen and fourteen years old, respectively, and they'd never seen anything like it.

Mark later recalled, "I heard the sirens Monday morning and at first didn't think much of it. But sirens are usually on Mountain Road and they pass by. These got closer and closer, so we looked down the street to see what was going on. We thought it was a house fire at first; then they started saying people were dead."

The news spread almost instantaneously. With cell phones and texting and instant messaging, by 10:30 a.m., less than a half hour after the arrests, most of the people of Cheshire knew that something very bad had happened.

As the crime scene was being processed, at least some of the cops on the scene were overcome by the magnitude of the crime. The CSIs who were documenting and gathering evidence knew what they were doing, but some of the younger police, who were guarding the perimeter to make sure the scene wasn't contaminated, were looking peaked.

For some, it was the first time they had ever been at the scene of a murder. There had been only three murders in Cheshire in the past ten years, and none of those was nearly as ghastly as this.

While there was still a buzz of activity at the Petit house, police went to Komisarjevsky's home. The house had once been impressive, but now it had fallen into disrepair. It had been many years since anyone had done any maintenance on this house. It couldn't have looked more out of place. All of its contemporaries had been torn down many years before. It had been named a historical site and therefore was untouchable. And so it had become an eyesore in a stretch of McMansions.

Though a book of local landmarks noted that the grounds· to the house once had a clay tennis court, those days were long gone. Now car parts and a backhoe covered the grounds. The house even lacked a front doorknob. Paper was stuffed into the hole where the doorknob had once been. A neighbor would later tell a reporter that the house had "been going downhill steadily for thirty years."

The woman who answered the door identified herself to police as Jude Komisarjevsky. She verified that she was Josh's mother. Police asked her if she knew where her son had been during the evening hours of July 22. She said that he was home from between approximately 7:30 p.m. until 11:30 p.m. At 11:30, she said, her son left to meet up with his friend Steve.

"Did he mentioned what their plans were?" an investigator asked.

"He said it was about a job."

"What was he wearing?"

"Dark clothing. A hooded sweatshirt," she replied, adding that, because of the time of night, she found his actions suspicious, and she hoped he wasn't getting himself into trouble again.

The woman allowed the policemen to have a quick look around and they noticed that Komisarjevsky's small daughter was living at the house. They also discovered that the family laptop computer was sitting on top of Joshua's bed. Mrs.

Komisarjevsky said that probably meant that her son had been using it before he went out. The investigators made a note to put the computer, a Compaq Presario 2100, on the list of items specifically mentioned on a search warrant.

Since both Komisarjevsky and Hayes had long histories of burglaries and larcenies, police felt there was a good chance that Komisarjevsky's computer activities before he went out had something to do with committing his crime. The subsequent search warrant said, "The investigators are aware that the World Wide Web contains websites that include information that provides detailed directions on how to restrain people, how to conceal, destruct, and alter evidence, as well as detailed accounts of criminal activities such as burglary, kidnapping, robbery, and arson."

There was also the possibility, the warrant said, that the computer contained information pertaining to plans Komisarjevsky and Hayes had made before they set out to burglarize the Petit home. The investigative team included members of the Connecticut State Police Computer Crime Unit, which had the resources, technology, and experience to examine the files on Komisarjevsky's laptop and make copies of any pertinent files.

After investigators had photographed the three bodies and thoroughly gone over the crime scene, the bodies were taken to the office of the Chief Medical Examiner. After the three sad autopsies were performed, the Medical Examiner determined, to no one's surprise, that the three had been victims of homicide. One had died from strangulation, while the other two had died from smoke inhalation.

Even before the questioning of Komisarjevsky and Hayes began, their clothes were seized. After investigators acquired a search warrant, the clothes were analyzed by scientists at the crime lab for evidence linking the two men to the crimes that had been committed against the Petits.

One such item was found immediately on Komisarjevsky's person: a pink cell phone, which was believed to have belonged to a member of the Petit family. A cell phone was also found in Hayes's pocket, a black Verizon phone.

The cell phone belonging to Komisarjevsky, which had been found lying in the middle of the road near the driver's side of the escape vehicle at the time of Komisarjevsky and Hayes's apprehension, was a Verizon cell phone in a black nylon case.

Just after midnight, a little more than fourteen hours after the murders, search warrants were granted to search the persons of the two arrested men, using a CT 100 Serchie Sexual Assault Evidence Collection Kit. The requests were made by detectives Christopher Consorte and Anthony Buglione of the Connecticut State Police Central District Major Crime Squad. Buglione's job was to investigate serious and violent crimes, including but not limited to murder. He had received special training in the collection of physical evidence, crime-scene processing, and the investigation of such cases.

The warrants allowed police investigators to search the bodies of the two suspects for "blood, saliva, semen, physiological fluids and secretions, hairs, fibers, fingerprints, palm prints, dust, dirt, accelerants, and items containing traces of the above-mentioned articles." If any of these substances or items were found, they were to be sent to the forensic laboratory for physical examination. Police, in other words, were looking for evidence that Komisarjevsky and Hayes had been in contact with members of the Petit family, specifically that sexual assaults may have occurred. Those tests would come back positive, indicating that both Hayes and Komisarjevsky had committed crimes of a sexual nature against their victims.

The two suspects were arraigned in a court in nearby Meriden.

As soon as the police blockade of Sorghum Mill Drive was removed, it began: A parade of cars crawled past the crime scene at pedestrian speed. In order to get to the Petit house from the main road, each car had to pass a sign that said, "Slow Down. We Love Our Children."

The curiosity seekers wanted to see the place where "it" happened. The spot where evil had laid its hand. It was evil you could see. The fire damage was visible. Many stopped and placed bouquets of flowers near the home—although they couldn't get too close because the area was still cordoned off by police tape. Three white bows were hung on trees in the yard. CSIs were still busy finishing up inside and outside the house.

Only family members were allowed to cross the tape. Jennifer's family had flown in from Pennsylvania as soon as they heard the news, and were allowed to sift through the ashes, looking for items that could be preserved. "We tried to gather up some things that may be of some value to us . . . but most of it's pretty well destroyed," Richard Hawke, Jennifer's father, told a TV reporter.

By Tuesday night police had finished processing the crime scene and turned the scorched house over to investigators from the Petits' insurance company. Only one police officer remained on the property to stand guard and make sure that those wishing to pay tribute to the family as well as curiosity seekers did not enter the house.

And the flowers kept coming. One woman who placed flowers on the growing memorial on Sorghum Mill Drive was Joan Morin, a patient of Dr. Petit. "It hits the heart," she said. "The family was just trying to live their life."

Kim Ferraiolo, who had lived next door to the Petits for three years, said, "They were the nicest people, just a great family. I last talked to Dr. Petit at 7:30 Sunday night and nothing seemed amiss. A neighbor alerted me to the fire on Monday morning, and I tried to call Dr. Petit at work but I was told he never showed. I'll always remember him tending his flowerbeds. He had a great sense of humor. I don't understand why they were picked. It's just hard to understand how someone could do something like that."

"They're just a lovely family," said the Reverend Ronald A. Rising, who for more than ten years had lived only a few houses away from the Petits. "It's just awful to think it would happen to a family like that in this community. You don't think about those things happening."

Reporters, too, were trying to sort it out in their brains. David Altimari of *The Hartford Courant* knew immediately that it was a horror story, but as the magnitude of it settled in, he realized it was "likely the worst crime that's ever been committed in Connecticut."

Driving around the Sorghum Mill Drive neighborhood, a reporter encountered two eleven-year-old boys. Asked their reaction to the news of the triple murder, one said, "I was seriously scared. I was freaked out."

One of Dr. Petit's patients, Nancy Manning of Rocky Hill, said, "It's a very sad day. The man's life is disintegrated now. His family was his life."

Helayne Lightstone, spokeswoman for the Hospital of Central Connecticut in New Britain where Dr. Petit worked, said that an employee prayer service for Dr. Petit would be held on Friday at noon, and that it would not be open to the public. "Grief counselors have been made available to our staff," Lightstone said.

Genevieve Haas at the Dartmouth College Office of Public Affairs officially announced that Hayley Petit, class of '11, had passed away, along with her sister and mother. The announcement noted that Hayley was the daughter of Dr. William Petit, class of '78.

The announcement said, "Hayley Petit, seventeen, was an accomplished athlete who had been recruited for Dartmouth's crew team and planned to row for the college as a first-year student in the fall of 2007." About Dr. Petit it added, "As a Dartmouth student, he was a member of the Alpha Chi Alpha fraternity and the Nathan Smith Society, a premedical organization for undergraduates. As an alumnus, Petit has been a longstanding supporter of the college." It concluded, "The Dartmouth College community joins William Petit in mourning for his loss," and gave an address for Dartmouth alumni to send their condolences.

At St. Mary's Hospital, where Dr. Petit had been taken to be treated for his head injuries, a New York City television reporter encountered Stephen Volpe, the Petit family's pastor at Cheshire United Methodist Church.

"He's doing okay physically," the pastor said. "Emotionally he is devastated and still worried about others." Volpe said that his church would be open at any hour for the next three days for those who needed to come and pray, meditate, or mourn. He said that certain details of the crimes against his family were being kept from Dr. Petit, but the pastor refused to elaborate.

Dr. Petit's father, William Petit Sr., said, "The totality and the reality and absolute finality of what happened is taking its toll."

The Petit family released its first statement to the public. It read, "Our precious family members have been the victims of horrible, senseless, violent assaults. We are understandably in shock and overwhelmed with sadness as we attempt to gather together to support one another and recognize these wonderful, giving, beautiful individuals who have been so cruelly taken from us."

On that Tuesday morning, Debbie Biggins—the woman who had been in the Bank of America the previous morning when Jennifer Hawke-Petit came in and passed the white slip of paper to the teller—turned on her computer to check the news.

It was only then, as she saw the headlines regarding the triple murder, that she realized the full impact of the events she had observed.

"I had been quite curious about what it was all about, but when I read the sad news it all fell into place," Biggins later recalled. She called the police and told them she had been a witness to the activities in the bank. She was subsequently interviewed by state troopers and a wide range of reporters, including one from *ABC News* who came to her home with a film crew.

Biggins said she felt a special empathy for Jennifer because she herself had been diagnosed with multiple sclerosis the previous May. It was the same disease that Jennifer had battled, the same disease that had prompted Jennifer and her daughters to launch a fundraising team to support MS research.

In the central Connecticut medical community, a different crisis arose: What to do with Dr. Petit's professional duties? Until Dr. Petit was able to resume practicing medicine, someone—or perhaps multiple someones—were going to have to fill his shoes.

And those were mighty big shoes. He was quite a bit more than just a local physician. He was a nationally known expert on diabetes. He had helped write several books. He was listed as a co-author of *The Natural Solution to Diabetes, The Encyclopedia of Diabetes,* and *The Encyclopedia of Endocrine Diseases and Disorders.*

In addition to his private practice and his book-writing career, he was the medical director of the Joslin Diabetes Center at the Hospital of Central Connecticut. He was also president of the Hartford County Medical Association. Other local endocrinologists were all willing to expand their schedules to take care of Dr. Petit's patients. But what of his job as the town of Plainville's health director?

Plainville Town Manager Robert E. Lee called Southington's health director, Charles I. Motes Jr., and asked him if he would be able to expand his territory. "I didn't even call Dr. Petit to ask," Lee recalled. "I just did it. I said, 'Hey, we have an issue here.' I called right away."

According to Lee the key responsibility of a health director is to review and sign legal orders about public health violations. The towns of Southington and Plainville had worked together in the past, running joint emergency health drills, for example.

"I received the call almost immediately after the tragedy," Dr. Motes recalled. "I was asked to consult and give advice to the town of Plainville in Dr. Petit's absence."

Judge Christina G. Dunnell set bond for both suspects at $15 million. She agreed to the high bonds recommended by officials because both of the suspects had lengthy criminal histories.

She then officially transferred the cases to New Haven Superior Court. The suspects were scheduled to appear in court on August 7.

It became the difficult job of Corrections Department Spokesman Brian Garnett to explain to the press why Hayes and Komisarjevsky had been free to kill despite those long records: Neither man had been convicted of a violent crime and both were deemed appropriate candidates for supervised parole. "Both were on a weekly reporting schedule with their parole officers and had been in full compliance with the requirements of their release, including being employed on a full-time basis," Garnett said.

Next to Cheshire itself, the central Connecticut community most profoundly impacted by the tragedy was Plainville, the town in which Dr. Petit had grown up. Fifteen miles north of Cheshire, Plainville had a population of 17,000.

Like Cheshire, Plainville was basically a crime-free community. The biggest event of the year was the annual hot-air balloon race. The town was where Dr. Petit still had his medical office. His father had served on the town council off and on from the late 1960s to the 1990s. Dr. Petit's sister, Johanna Chapman, was currently on the council.

Deborah Tom, who ran a sign shop in town and was president of the local Rotary Club, told a *New York Times* reporter, "You think of Plainville, and you think of the Petits."

"Everybody is stunned—beyond stunned," said Christopher J. Wazorko, who served on the Plainville town council. "We're all having a difficult time putting into words what we're feeling," he said. "You see some of these things on TV. It happens in other communities, in other states. And this one has hit pretty close to home."

Law enforcement and the governing bodies of Connecticut were thrown by the magnitude of the crimes. Those who were politicians, whose careers depended on winning elections, scrambled to act quickly, to say just the right thing, to calm nerves, to keep residents from panicking. Cheshire Town Manager Michael Milone admitted to being befuddled. "The only thing we are trying to do is get the neighborhood back to some degree of normalcy. I don't know the response. We're not trained in something like this," Milone said.

And so those who *were* trained were called in. Grief counselors from around the region were sent into the crisis zone, psychologists trained in preserving the mental health of communities traumatized by unthinkable tragedies.

From the cauldron of fear and sadness bubbled anger. Why were the killers among us in the first place? State Senator Sam Caligiuri of Waterbury wrote Robert Farr, the chairman of the Connecticut Board of Pardons and Parole, and said, "Three people are dead and the suspects were judged by the state's parole board just a few months ago to be appropriate candidates for early supervised release. We owe it to the victims, their families and friends, and to the public to find out why these suspects were seen as ready for supervised parole and what action the state can take to prevent such a horrific thing from happening again."

Connecticut Governor M. Jodi Rell ordered an assessment of all the procedures that relate to how suspects are charged, sentenced, and released. She appointed a panel to review key steps in the justice system.

State officials announced that they were "re-examining policies" regarding letting repeat offenders out of prison on parole. Robert Farr said that Hayes and Komisarjevsky were out on parole for one simple reason: Neither suspect had a history of violence.

"That's why this is sort of shocking—because it doesn't fit a normal mode," Farr said. "I'll admit that the board didn't have as much information as it should have about the men's records, such as the transcript of a Bristol Court hearing in which a judge called Komisarjevsky a 'cold-blooded, calculating predator.' They were obviously individuals that had long and extensive records, but they weren't violent records."

Some thought, "Yes, no violence, but when you break into homes in the middle of the night, isn't the threat of violence always there?" Didn't the threat of violence count as violence? It did in an armed robbery.

State Senator Sam Caligiuri, whose district included the town of Cheshire, said, "I think the entire parole process seems to be in a shambles. According to the current rules, neither suspect had any history of violent crimes, but I think the rules should be changed. Many of my constituents feel burglary is a violent crime. You are breaking into someone's private domain. It should be their sanctuary."

New Haven State's Attorney Michael Dearington said it was too early for him to discuss the death penalty, although he was aware that public opinion leaned heavily in that direction. "I know the public consensus is they should be fried tomorrow," Dearington said.

Anger was so ripe that vigilantes were a concern. Department of Corrections Spokesman Brian Garnett noted that the prisoners were separated from both each other and the general prison population. Hayes was being held at Northern Correctional Institution in Somers, while Komisarjevsky was at the MacDougall–Walker Correctional Institution in Suffield.

The two men had met in one halfway house and then had become friends when they were transferred together to a second segue between prison and the free world. Robert Pidgeon, chief executive officer of Community Solutions Inc., which ran both facilities, said, "There's nobody that would have predicted this."

The Cheshire murders made the national news. Short segments on the evening news were featured on ABC, NBC, and CBS. On cable, the twenty-four-hour news stations were giving the case more extensive treatment.

MSNBC's crime commentator, Clint Van Zandt, a former FBI profiler, was among the most eloquent when speaking of Cheshire's nightmare.

"If I've learned one thing in my forty years of investigative experience, it's to never believe that you've seen the limits of man's inhumanity to man," Van Zandt said.

He noted that the residents of the Petits' neighborhood had been lulled into a false sense of security because criminals hadn't struck there before. Emergency calls to that area were most apt to concern a chimney fire or a fender bender.

The cruelty of the Petit murders reminded Van Zandt of similar horrific crimes from the past. The first example that occurred to him was the 1959 murder of four members of the Clutter family—Herb and Bonnie, and their children Kenyon and Nancy. That crime, memorialized by author Truman Capote in his book *In Cold Blood*, took place in a small town in Kansas. The murderers, Dick Hickock and Perry Smith, had believed that the Clutters had a safe full of money. When Hickock and Smith discovered that the money didn't exist, they bound the four family members, cut their throats, and shot each in the head with a shotgun. The crime netted the pair $41. Despite the fact that they left no witnesses, they were captured and tried in a court of law. It took a jury less than two hours to convict them and sentence them to death.

Van Zandt said the Petit murders also reminded him of the New Year's Day 2006 murder of the Harvey family in Richmond, Virginia. In that case two burglars named Ricky Gray and Ray Dandridge entered the Harvey home through an open door and murdered Bryan and Kathryn Harvey as well as their daughters, four-year-old Ruby and nine-year-old Stella. Gray and Dandridge had been seeking a house to rob. Their crime netted only a couple of hundred dollars' worth of items, but their savagery was startling. The victims were beaten to death with a hammer, their throats cut, and the house set ablaze in an attempt to cover up the crime. The pair, it turned out, had been responsible for nine murders in total, including that of one of the killer's ex-wives.

Van Zandt predicted that psychologists would spend many hours trying to figure out what made Hayes and Komisarjevsky tick, just as psychologists had examined and analyzed all of the sociopathic killers that came before them. The doctors would try to figure out the question that so haunted central Connecticut: Why?

Did it really matter why? Van Zandt concluded that it did. "We need to understand the motivation of such killers to help us better understand the future crimes by other sociopaths, psychotics, and antisocial personalities," he said.

But can something as senseless as the Petit murders ever be truly understood? Maybe not. Not by people of conscience, anyway. Crimes this brutal give the most experienced and hardened homicide detectives nightmares. Van Zandt knew what he was talking about.

In Cheshire, Van Zandt believed a "perfect storm" of two sociopaths caused the tragedy. Hayes was not a sophisticated guy, but Komisarjevsky was young and smart, a man who envisioned himself as capable of greatness in the criminal world. They preyed off of each other, goaded each other on, and together became capable of atrocity.

Dr. James Monahan, a professor of criminal justice, told WCVB-TV in Boston that he believed drugs played a major part in the crime. "Drugs such as cocaine or meth," he said. "These kind of drugs are associated with superhuman, ultraviolent actions."

Another factor was the age difference between Hayes and Komisarjevsky. "I see an older con taking the young one under his wing and teaching him the ropes," Dr. Monahan said. "This could be much like the case of the Washington, DC, snipers. Komisarjevsky and Hayes made a deadly pair even though neither had a violent history. With the snipers, they didn't have much of a criminal history at all, but they paired up and became superviolent in a way that, if you separated them, you wouldn't have seen."

Chapter 4:

"I Sure Am Glad That I Didn't Run into Him"

By July 26, 2007, the numbness began to wear off and the true horror began to sink in for Connecticut residents. Using court documents, reporters located some of Josh Komisarjevsky's previous burglary victims. One was Charles Turnier of Burlington, one of nineteen homeowners who had been burglarized by Joshua Komisarjevsky during 2002. Of those nineteen burglaries, ten took place in Bristol, two in Burlington, six in Cheshire, and one in Farmington. All of the houses were within a short distance of Komisarjevsky's home, and the modus operandi was always the same. He would climb into the house at night through a cut window screen or an unlocked sliding door. In each case mostly electronic items and cash were stolen.

"When my house was burglarized," Turnier said. "I was living there with my then-pregnant wife. I noticed that the cellar door was open. I looked over and all my electronics were stolen. He stole a very large knife from me. I sure am glad that I didn't run into him," Turnier said. "Later, police told me that Komisarjevsky had said that he had been watching my family for days before the crime. When police questioned him he told them that he had studied our routine by hiding in the bushes. He knew when my wife was home and when she had left the home. It's haunting, knowing that a lifelong criminal was in my home, just a few feet away from my family while I slept. My heart goes out to the Petit family, but I'm thankful it didn't happen to my wife."

The Petit home was the third that had been broken into that weekend by Hayes and Komisarjevsky. The instant Komisarjevsky's parole officer removed his electronic tracing device, he went on a breaking-and-entering spree, just like an addict goes on a binge—and he took his partner in crime Hayes along for the ride. And so, among the most stunned and frightened of the locals were the homeowners who had been burglarized by the pair only hours before the Petit murders. One of those homeowners was Ronald Bergamo Jr., who lived three miles from the Petits. Exactly one day before Hayes and Komisarjevsky broke into the Petit home, they had broken in Bergamo's.

When police told him who the culprits were, Bergamo admitted he was shaken. "We were within twenty-four hours of being that family," Bergamo said.

The men had entered his home as he slept beside his wife. Also asleep in the house were his twelve-year-old son and another couple. The burglars entered through an unlocked door and took only cash. Bergamo knew that something was wrong on Sunday morning when he saw that the intruders had left a large carving knife on a table in the family room.

Bergamo took a moment and thought about the long-term effects that the murders were going to have on his community. Cheshire, he feared, had been changed forever. "We're not that quaint town anymore," he said.

The other house that Hayes and Komisarjevsky entered that weekend was on the same street as Bergamo's and belonged to David Hick. Hick's home was also entered during the early morning hours of Sunday, July 22. The burglars took cash, credit cards, a cell phone, and—most disturbingly—a photo of Hicks and his wife.

"The taking of the photo made us wonder if the robbers planned on targeting us," Hicks said. "That's one thing that is really bothering us. What happened to them [the Petits] could have happened to us."

An Associated Press reporter contacted Glenn Petit, Dr. Petit's brother, who was forthcoming with some details that police had told him. How had the murderers picked the Petits as their victims?

Glenn Petit said, "They were attracted to the car. They liked the car, followed her home, thought she lived in a nice house."

How was his brother doing?

"He's doing as well as can be expected," the brother said. "Emotionally, he's a mess. He is stunned right now. He's had his family taken from him."

Bob Averack, who lived across the street from the Petits, was asked by a reporter how it felt to live so close. He admitted that it had been a shattering experience, even for those in proximity to it.

"What all of them went through, especially that little Michaela. It completely broke me up," Averack said. "The anger and the sadness and the absolute outrage at what happened to that family is beyond description. As a husband and as a father, you want to be there to preserve and protect the ones you love, and when you're placed in the powerless position of not being able to do that, it's very profound."

In addition to talking to as many friends and family members of the victims as they could find, reporters were also seeking comments from the families of the murderers.

The Komisarjevskys, a family with a storied history that offered nothing to prepare them for this moment, issued a statement: "It was a monstrous, deranged act, beyond comprehension. We cannot and will not condone anything the accused have done. Justice needs to take place. We can add nothing more—simply to repeat how tragic this is and how much our thoughts and prayers go out to the Petit family and friends. Our sympathy goes to the victims and to all those whose lives they touched. We're so sorry that anything like this could happen. We sincerely hope that Dr. Petit fully recovers from his wounds. The police are in charge of the case. We support them in their task."

The message was delivered by Josh's uncle Christopher Komisarjevsky, the former chief executive of the prominent public relations firm Burson-Marsteller.

The family of Steven Hayes released a statement to the media that read, "Three families are suffering, and the pain is too much to bear for anyone affected by this unforgivable act."

Equally shocked were the residents of Wilderness Way in the Nelson Farms section of Bristol, where Komisarjevsky had briefly lived. Like Deaconwood, Nelson Farms was an upscale housing development with plenty of trees.

During the time he lived on that street, back in 2001, Komisarjevsky had burglarized ten homes. One woman awoke to him in her house and screamed hysterically until he fled. He had eventually been caught and served time, but the news that he had been let free and had become a murderer was chilling to those in the Bristol neighborhood.

"To find out that, here we were concerned about break-ins, and it was someone in our own community," said one

Wilderness Way woman. "We have neighborhoods around here with a higher crime rate. To hear that it was someone who lived here was just shocking."

As details of the crimes continued to leak out little by little, authorities took the unusual step of urging people not to believe everything they read and heard. Chief Cruess issued a written statement encouraging the community to view all news reports with "a healthy dose of skepticism."

Cruess noted that with such a flood of media attention, there were bound to be mistakes. "Not all of the information has been correct, and I ask everyone to take this into consideration when reading or viewing these items," he said. "Unfortunately, with the investigation still actively ongoing, we are unable to provide some of the information which the community is seeking so that we do not jeopardize the investigation. Cheshire residents should rest assured that all the suspects in this case have been apprehended and are currently in the custody of the Connecticut Department of Correction."

The rumor the chief was trying to squelch was that more than two men had attacked the Petit home and that some were still running around free. This rumor had apparently started because of the factual report that the two vehicles involved in the home invasion had been found in Quarry Village and the Maplecroft Plaza parking lot, respectively. Unaware that the killers had used the Petit's SUV during the attack, some wondered how the two men got from those locations to the crime scene.

Reporters Luther Turmelle and Phil Helsel theorized in the July 26 edition of *The Journal Register* that Hayes and Komisarjevsky had walked from the Quarry Village Apartments to the Petit house carrying the containers of gasoline they used to set the house on fire. This theory was not wholly satisfactory because it begs the question, if the men had to carry heavy containers of gas, why didn't they find a spot closer to the Petit home to park Komisarjevsky's car?

Police could have quieted these troubling whispers by announcing that the pair had used the Petits' SUV to pick up the containers of gas during the night, and at that point had moved their own vehicle further away from the crime scene. Hayes had returned to his car sometime during the night, probably during the gasoline run, to drop off items he had stolen from the house. But it was the inclination of police, especially with the investigation ongoing, to give the public less rather than more information, so people were left wondering about the movements of the two men and possible accomplices.

Despite assurances from police and community leaders that this was an isolated incident, that the perpetrators had been caught, and that everyone in central Connecticut was perfectly safe, Cheshire residents could practically taste the fear in the air.

"You walk around town and you can see the fear on people's faces," said Cheshire Police Lieutenant Jay Markella.

The closer people lived to the Petit home, the worse it was. Jill Veiga, the Petits' next-door neighbor, said, "Since this happened, I'm afraid to go into my basement at night."

Chapter 5:

Komisarjevsky and Hayes

So who were the two lowlifes who committed these crimes? A look at their backgrounds revealed some surprises. For one thing, Josh Komisarjevsky, the younger of the two, came from an accomplished family. His past behavior was also such that the tragedy at the Petit house *might* have been predicted.

Josh was the adopted son of a blue-blooded family, a family that had lived in Cheshire for many generations, a family that had been, as they say, "prominent in the arts." He was adopted when he was only two weeks old by a couple who believed that they could not have children of their own.

They were truly blue-blooded, as in royal. Josh's great-grandfather Fyodor sang opera in Russia and married a princess. Their son, Theodore, was a theater director said to have put on some of the all-time great productions of Shakespeare's *King Lear* and of the works of Chekhov. Theodore married Ernestine Stodelle, a dancer.

When Theodore passed away in 1954, Ernestine remarried. Her second husband was John Chamberlain, a celebrated newsman and syndicated writer. Chamberlain was known for his conservative columns. He owned a pre-Revolutionary War home in Cheshire, with its own wishing well and sixty-five acres of land. The home, an official Cheshire Landmark, was known as the Merriman Cook House, after the man who had built it in 1768. That was the same house that now had newspaper shoved in the hole where the front-door doorknob used to be.

Josh's uncle, Christopher Komisarjevsky, once told the *New York Times*, "My mother was a beautiful, avant-garde dancer who danced with the seminal dancers of modern dance, and my father had left Russia at the time of the revolution to escape the Communists and directed theater in London and in New York. That was the kind of environment we grew up in."

It was in that house that Josh spent many of his formative years. His parents were Benedict Komisarjevsky, who owned a construction company, and the former Jude Motyka. Josh had a sister, Naomi. Jude home-schooled both children. Home-schooling Josh was a hard task, as he suffered from a variety of learning disabilities.

A very religious couple, Benedict and Jude took in foster children over the years, many of whom had problems often found in children who move from place to place, living in a system rather than a real home.

A turning point in Josh's life came when he was fourteen and his grandfather, John Chamberlain, died. That was 1995. Three other things happened that same year.

First, Josh learned that he was adopted.

Second, he was raped by one of the foster children living in the house. We know this is so because Jude reported the incident to the Connecticut State Department of Children and Families.

Third, he began to break into houses. Breaking and entering is a vice that often becomes addictive and can escalate into more severe crimes.

A neighbor who remembered Josh as a boy had no idea that he had been a troubled kid. "The only mischief I can recall Joshua stirring up as a child in the 1980s was when he and his friends scuffed the clay tennis court behind his grandparents' home with their tricycles."

As a teenager, Josh acquired a drug habit. He committed burglaries to feed his habit.

According to his uncle Christopher, "The kid was in and out of trouble. He was estranged from the family."

For that one year between 2001 and 2002, Josh had moved out of his parents' house and was living with his seventeen-year-old girlfriend, Jennifer Norton, at 150 Wilderness Way in the Nelson Farms section of Bristol. The Bristol neighborhood was subsequently plagued by a series of burglaries. Josh was arrested for the first time at age twenty-one, on March 11, 2002, and charged with burglarizing ten Bristol homes. He was also charged with burglarizing two homes in Burlington in March 2001, six in Cheshire in May 2001, and one in Farmington in November 2001. Local police described him as a cat burglar who always worked close to his home, which was in Cheshire. He worked alone and always entered houses at night while the residents were asleep. He entered the houses from the back, cutting a window screen and crawling inside. He primarily stole high-end electronics such as DVD players and stereos, but also took women's purses and cash if they were readily available. One unusual technique he used was to wear night vision goggles. Police did not know how he got the goggles, which could have cost him as much as $2,000.

One of his targets turned out to be, coincidentally, the home of a state trooper. Komisarjevsky came upon the trooper's uniform. He stole some shirts and the peace officer's hat. He later claimed to have given those items away.

According to New Britain court records, Komisarjevsky and his teenage girlfriend had a daughter named Jayda in March 2002. Jayda's mother, Jennifer Norton, was seventeen when the baby was born. Komisarjevsky, twenty-one, missed the birth because he was in jail. He had been arrested after he pawned stolen items. State police, working in conjunction with local police, noticed the similarities between the burglaries in the different towns.

Jennifer later recalled, "He was always out. He told me stories about jobs that he had or that he had done or, you know, robbing houses. When I was pregnant he was abusive and never around. He was doing coke and crystal meth.

"He loved the adrenaline rush and thrill of it. He said, 'Robbing a house is better than any drug I've ever tried.' Later, after he was arrested, they searched my house and they found so much stuff [that he had stolen] in the basement."

A picture of Josh and Jennifer was taken one Halloween. They were dressed as Bonnie and Clyde. Another picture showed the young Josh with a joint tucked behind his ear. He liked the excitement of crime. Robbing a house when no one was home was boring.

On September 17, 2002, Komisarjevsky appeared in District Court in Bristol and pleaded guilty to several of the charges against him. The agreement that was submitted to the court at that time was a split sentence with a cap of ten years on the executed portion of the sentence. Komisarjevsky had previously pleaded guilty to separate charges in a Meriden court with a cap of five years. During that hearing the state reserved the right to argue at a later date that Komisarjevsky serve consecutive time.

Because of subsequent events, Joshua Komisarjevsky's sentencing hearing on December 20, 2002, in District Court in Bristol is worth close scrutiny. Presiding was the Honorable James M. Bentivegna. Prosecuting the case was Ronald Dearstyne for the state. Defending Komisarjevsky was attorney William Gerace.

After establishing that the proceedings were getting under way in the afternoon because attorneys on both sides had other business that morning, the judge greeted Josh.

"Good afternoon, Your Honor," the defendant said.

The judge asked if Komisarjevsky's parents were in the courtroom and was informed that they were. Gerace asked if it was okay for the parents to stand behind their son. The judge said he wasn't comfortable with that because of possible security issues and agreed instead to let the parents sit in the front row of the spectator area behind their son.

Dearstyne told the court that he had read all of the police reports regarding Komisarjevsky's crimes, then added:

> *These are not only burglaries, but they are very serious burglaries. In my almost fifteen years as a prosecutor and my eight years as a cop, I will tell the court—and I'm sure the court knows this already—that most home burglaries occur during the day, not at nighttime. That's basically for this reason: People who break into houses prefer to do it when no one is home. They basically do not want to be confronted by homeowners. However, that is an exception in this defendant's case, because in all of these cases, except for the one involving the car break, they all occurred during the nighttime.*
>
> *Mr. Komisarjevsky appears before the court today. He has a record in Meriden, of course. But at the time these were committed, he basically had no record. And I will tell the court that he did assist the police departments—or the troopers—in this investigation. When the police came to his house with two warrants, he gave himself up for everything, eighteen burglaries in all. He confessed to everything, even the crimes that had been committed the summer before. The state trooper talked to the prosecutor about how cooperative*

he had been but he was incarcerated anyway and missed his daughter's birth.

That said, I should also point out that Mr. Komisarjevsky only cooperated with the police after he was caught. It was not as if he woke up one morning, realized suddenly that he had done something wrong, and turned himself in, saying, "Here I am and here is what I have done."

He pretty much copped out to these other crimes after he was arrested on two warrants already. As far as the costs, when we finish here today, there will be cost that we will be able to quantify, and there will be a cost to this defendant, and the terms of how much time he will have to spend in jail for these offenses, how much time he may be on probation, whatever conditions the court may impose.

So, by the end of this afternoon, within the next fifteen or twenty minutes—I'm going to use the word cost—we will know what the cost is to Mr. Komisarjevsky for these crimes that he committed here. We know what the numerical or the monetary loss or cost is to the victims. If my addition is correct—and I did use a calculator, but I've been known to mess that up—it came to $25,369 in losses. That's according to the victims who responded. We have a number of victims who did not respond.

And while I'm on the point, I'd like to ask the court that, in regards to the victims who did not respond, the state would ask the court not to draw any conclusions from that either way for this reason: Perhaps they didn't respond because they didn't want to be heard, or perhaps they didn't respond because they were fearful. We don't know.

The other cost is one that is not as easily quantified. And that is the emotional trauma suffered by these people, the trauma that they will have to live with probably for the rest of their lives. And that is why the State sees this type of crime as a crime against a person, not a crime against property. A lot of people seem to think that theft and breaking into homes is a crime against property. In fact, it's not really a crime against property; it's a crime against the people who live in those homes.

One victim stated, in part, "The defendant should get as much jail time as possible." As a result of the incident, he stated that he and his wife have installed an alarm system for $600, plus the monthly fee, as a result of the incident.

So these people, as a result of this crime, apparently do not feel safe in their home. They went out and put in a new alarm system. And his wife still feels unsafe when he goes to work early in the morning. He indicated that it's not right that someone should feel unsafe on their own property. And I totally agree with him. If you can't feel safe in your own home at night, where can you feel safe?

Another victim tells us that she was missing $40 in cash and her license and her passport as a result of the incident. She stated that she invested in an alarm system as a result of the incident, which cost $450 to install. Here's another victim who went out and had an alarm system installed in an attempt to make them feel safer.

She stated, "I haven't slept through the night since this happened. I know he's locked up, but I still think someone's trying to get into my house. He stole things instead of getting a job cutting lawns or at McDonald's, and has no regard for his victims. We all have consequences for our actions. I request that he be given the most jail time possible. Someone like him should not be on the street."

She will have to suffer this emotional trauma probably for the rest of her life. She no longer feels safe in her home.

Now we move on to yet another victim. This one states that he did not put in a claim with his insurance company and that he installed an alarm in his house after the incident. What makes this particular incident very aggravating is the following: He stated that there were four children in the house that night, and they were really frightened after the incident.

He said, "We were just glad that he didn't go upstairs where the kids were. The kids would have loved to have gotten their things back sooner from the police department, but they are glad he was caught and he is going to serve jail time."

These victims did not make a statement regarding the amount of jail time they wished to see the defendant receive. But in this case we do not just have adults who will live in fear, but children as well, who will feel fear for the rest of their lives, or at least as long as they live in that house. And they will be afraid because of what this man did, not just breaking into their home, but breaking into their home during the nighttime as they slept.

Let's move on to another victim. This man said that he would be willing to have the defendant serve less jail time if it meant that he would get his money back sooner. He said that his wife was in a wheelchair and that they have been on a budget ever since he retired. He said that he did not notice the money missing from his wallet until he went to the store to buy something and discovered that it was not there.

That represents just a handful of the victims we have in this group of cases. With regard to the victims, Mr. Komisarjevsky has said, "I wish I could tell them that I am sorry. I can't even imagine how violated they must feel. I wish there was something I could do." And of course, he has no understanding of how violated these people feel in their homes. He goes on to say, "I live with this fact. I live with this wrong every day. I keep hearing from the prosecutor that I am a wild animal. I am not." I want to clarify for the record that, in my recollection, I have never referred to this defendant as a wild animal. I've had no reason to do that. And that terminology would be wrong.

On the other hand, I do think he is a dangerous person who poses a danger to the State of Connecticut, and as a result should be punished severely for what he's done here.

The defendant says that he had to break into these homes in order to pay back his drug dealer. I have here the statement that he gave the police, which runs down how he broke into all of the homes, and where those houses were located. I won't read the whole thing because it is quite lengthy. But there are a couple of things that I want to point out, because it shows his planning, it shows his awareness, it shows that he [knew] what he was doing. In the state's view, it shows that he was not high on drugs when he committed these crimes, that he was very aware of the situation around him, that he was prepared to commit these crimes, and that he was not a novice breaking into someone's house.

In his statement he states, "I wore latex gloves for all of these. I tried not to do any damage, and I didn't want to see any of the people in the houses. I started doing these in July and August, but stopped when it got cold. I also had a job around then, so I didn't need to do this."

So he tells us a couple of things in that part of his statement. One, he knew to wear gloves so that he wouldn't leave behind fingerprints. He tried not to do any damage. He knew, by his own admission, that there were people in these houses. And, even if he didn't know, he could assume that people would be home during the nighttime.

He also told us that he had a job. That contradicts his statement that he committed these crimes to pay back his drug dealer. Here he states that he was employed and did not have to steal.

Now here is part of his statement in which he shows how he planned out his crimes. He said, "Sometime between two and three weeks ago I was in the town of Burlington, Connecticut, in [friend] Ryan Ludwig's neighborhood. I was alone in the neighborhood and parked my Toyota pickup truck on the grass near Ryan's driveway so that Ryan and his parents would be unable to see the vehicle if they looked out of the house. I then walked through several front yards to get a feel for the neighborhood and make sure that no one was around. I then went to a residence across the street from Ryan Ludwig's house. The house had a yellow Dodge pickup truck in the driveway. I then went to the rear of the house and located an unlocked sliding glass door. I then opened the door and listened. Without entering their house, I then stayed in the door area for approximately ten or fifteen minutes. I could hear someone breathing loudly, so I left the area without shutting the door."

This is a cool, collected person who is not showing, in the State's view, any nervousness breaking into these houses. Later in his statement he says, "The room where I entered was some type of den and office combination. I opened the sliding glass door to make a quick escape should I need one. I know there was a television on upstairs, so I did not go there. I noticed a newer, good computer on a nice wood desk in the same room where I entered. I began to disassemble the computer. I needed to take two trips to the truck before leaving. I think I left the door open. I also left the window open."

He is not a person who is breaking into these houses, going in, grabbing stuff, and leaving. He is looking in before he goes in. When he gets in, he's checking out the area to see what's going on around him. He then has no problem spending time there, taking apart computers. In this particular *case, not only does he go in once and take stuff, he goes back in to take more stuff.*

His statement continues, "*Several nights later I went back to Ryan Ludwig's neighborhood, planning to break into the same house where I heard the person sleeping. I parked my truck in Ryan's driveway and walked across the street. I went to the back of the house I had previously been at. I opened the rear sliding door and stood in the door area and listened for approximately ten or fifteen minutes. I didn't hear anything so I entered the home.*" And he goes on to describe the items that he took. He then says, "*I left the house at approximately 4:30 a.m. I was walking back to my truck when a female started a car in the driveway of the residence. I then sat in the bushes until she left, for approximately five or ten minutes. The female left in the car. I then went back to my truck and left the area.*"

And then, in the last paragraph of his statement, the defendant says, "*The first time I ever broke into a house was when I was fourteen years old in Cheshire, Connecticut. This was a nighttime burglary. I always broke into houses during the night, never during the day. After breaking into houses between the ages of fourteen and sixteen, I stopped. All of the houses were in Cheshire, and I stopped because I got caught. I started up again due to a lack of money and a job. I always wore gloves, with the exception of one incident when I was fourteen. I always acted alone. Approximately a year and a half ago I acquired some night-vision goggles. I took them from a friend of mine who had stolen some of my military equipment. I used the night-vision equipment during the burglaries during the past year. I also used the green army backpack that is now in my room to carry my tools, night-vision, and knives used to cut the screen. I always avoided contact with people.*"

So now we learn that the defendant is in possession of night-vision equipment, which allows him to walk into a dark house and pretty much see what is going on, see every-thing in that house. So, even if a homeowner happened to come down into a dark room, this individual, in all likeli-hood, would be able to see that homeowner, where the home-owner probably wouldn't be able to see him if it were dark enough. Again, that shows preparation, a coolness that adds to the seriousness of these crimes. In fifteen years of handling burglary cases I can't recall a person planning it out to this degree.

Some people, when they start down the road of criminal activity, they take small steps to begin with, but this defen-dant entered the world of criminal activity with one heck of a big step. He jumped right in. It's not like he stuck his toe in the water to try it out. He knew what he was doing, and he endangered the lives of many, many people. Fortunately, no one has been hurt physically. But they sure have been hurt emotionally. A physical pain is going to go away after a while. But in these cases I'm not sure if the emotional pain is ever going to go away.

Dearstyne then requested a total of thirty years suspended after ten years to serve, not to run consecutive to Komisar-jevsky's Meriden cases. That sentence, the prosecutor argued, "punishes him, and allows these victims to have some peace and comfort for a period of time, and allows him when he gets out of jail in the future, and he will get out of jail, to be on probation for a period of time and hopefully make some restitution."

Then it was Gerace's turn to argue for leniency. He began, "Your honor, what the prosecutor has just indicated is all correct. It is a terrible thing to have your home burglarized. I have never been that unfortunate, but I can imagine the residual effects are tremendous. That being said, I would like to stress the fact that the magnitude of Mr. Komisarjevsky's problems are from his own mouth. I mention that, Judge, because the first step toward rehabilitation is to acknowledge what you have done and how bad you have been." Gerace described how Komisarjevsky had driven around with police to point out all of the houses he remembered breaking into, even cruising around searching when he couldn't remember the exact street. He continued:

> *For the burglaries in Meriden, Judge [Earl] Richards gave Josh three years to serve, with six years' special parole. And I wasn't his lawyer. Attorney [Gregory] St. John from Waterbury was, and he handled that. But the motivating factor there was to get the cases over with. They knew the enormity of the situation. They knew he was going to be sentenced here.*
>
> *Josh has a history, Judge, that is really different, terribly disturbing. His family is here today. Here are just the salient points in his past. When Josh was fourteen, four people close to him died, including his grandfather, his counselor. He learned that he was adopted, and, according to his parents, that was traumatic for him. He suffers from ADD, dyslexia, and dysgraphia. Dysgraphia is a learning disability resulting from difficulty in expressing thoughts in writing and graphing. It generally refers to extremely poor handwriting. So he has three severe learning disabilities. Notwithstanding that, he's a very smart young man. He's very capable with his hands. As you saw, he was able to disassemble a computer and put it back together.*

His spotty work history is not spotty in the sense that he was bad on the job. Every one of his employers, I think, said that he is able to work. He was consistent. He only stopped showing up when he, on a couple of occasions, had a suicide attempt or a drug overdose, and was unable to continue or didn't choose to continue at the job. But he's able to be employed.

He, despite his learning disabilities, can be a productive member of society. And I think the issue that Your Honor has to grapple with is how much of a punishment is appropriate. Certainly, general deterrence has to be served. These people have to know. And people out there who are thinking of burglarizing have to know that you'll be punished.

But Josh has been in jail for some period of time now. He's been doing dead time since his sentence in Meriden, which was some four months ago. Josh, is that right?

"Yes," Komisarjevsky said.

Gerace continued:

Any day in jail is too much for some people. Any hour in jail is too much for most people. So I don't know how much jail it takes to deter someone from doing something like this. I have a feeling that someone who is going to break into a house at nighttime isn't going to be deterred by someone else, because it's just a bizarre and erratic thing to do. A rational thought process can't be part of the formula that person is using to think this through. I say this because Joshua has had eight concussions. He has been in Elmcrest Hospital and, in my view, should have stayed there.

His family is very spiritual. When he was prescribed anti-depressive medication, his parents thought that that was a crutch. They felt that it was a weakness of some sort and that he should deal with his depression on a spiritual level.

When he was in Elmcrest, where he most likely could have benefited from some attention to whatever deficits he has, mentally and emotionally, he was taken out of there and brought to a faith program in Vermont or New Hampshire. So, at each juncture, when Josh could have and should have gotten psychiatric and/or psychotropic medication, I think his parents in good faith thought that they could spiritually handle the situation. And I'm not being critical of them. I'm just wondering that had they not made that choice, if Josh would have degenerated or not. I don't know the answer to that.

But it's clearly something very wrong, because the state hit on something else. These burglaries, although they may have been a vehicle for him to buy drugs, were carefully planned, and he has a photographic memory. And he took the police to every house and he knew what he took from each house, which is a scary, scary thing to contemplate.

So what I'm trying to suggest to the court is that there's a mental abnormality here or psychiatric problem that needs to be addressed, over and above the drug abuse and drug addiction. So whatever remedy the court fashions, I'm asking the court to consider that Josh obviously has a twisted psyche. I think it is a mental aberration that compels him to commit these crimes in the first place, and secondly to remember it and feel compelled at some point to unburden himself with all the details. Mr. Dearstyne is right. People who are junkies, they smash the window, they run in, and they grab the stereo, and they run out the door. So there's much more to this. This young man, Judge, has parents who are still sticking with him. He has stated that he thought he had burned those bridges, and he is surprised that they still support him. They do love him very much. His girlfriend is here with his little child who he has held just once since she was born. He has a lack of insight, obviously, into his problems.

I would also like to point out that Josh has been having a difficult time in jail. The court may be aware he's in protective custody. All kinds of things have happened to him. You know that, sexually, he was abused at several different levels at various points in his life. That again started out with foster children in the home, the parents trying to be good people.

I don't know if any of this is the reason or the cause. I'm pointing them out because something went wrong with Josh. He is twenty-two years old. This is his first go about with the criminal justice system.

He's done terrible things. If you want to itemize it and stack it up, he should be doing thirty years. But he did not commit these crimes one a year for many years, Your Honor. You have to understand, he committed these crimes in a flurry of activity.

His parents would like to address you at this juncture, Judge. If they may be allowed to come forward.

"All right," the judge said.

After the parents announced their full names for the record, Komisarjevsky's mother spoke first:

I think if you read in one of the cases, you'd see that one of the detectives had called our house looking for Joshua. He identified himself as being from the Motor Vehicle Department, but my caller ID told me otherwise. I called Joshua and let him know, "You must be in trouble. They are looking for you." And Josh knew they were coming and stayed right there. So he was not running. He was not trying to hide. He had made up his mind at that point that his life was in trouble and he needed to cooperate. He decided to cooperate with the police. It was his drug problems. That's why he lost all of his employments, because of his drug problems. And, as Attorney Gerace brought up, he did have abusive problems when he was a child that led to his depression. We didn't take him out of Elmcrest. He was released. That was all they would do with him at that point.

We did refuse the drugs because Joshua wanted them. He wanted to overdose with them. And we did seek other treatments. Most of the time they just kicked him out and told him he was worthless. And he has shown sorrow to us in all the times that we had visited him. And he even went so far as to invite young people to come to court today to see what has happened to him so they won't make the wrong choice too.

With that, Mrs. Komisarjevsky concluded her statement. "All right, thank you," the judge said.

Then it was Josh's father's turn to speak:

My name is Ben Komisarjevsky. Thank you for this honor of coming before you, speaking for my son. We have stood by our son for all these years, and we do love him and care about him, and consider him as our true son even though he was adopted.

And my wife and I weren't able to have children, so we went and got Joshua when he was fourteen days old. And it's been a privilege to have him as a son since then and to walk all the trials and the tribulations that we have experienced.

And i.e., of his own speaking that came out of his mouth, which we have taught him over the years to be truthful, this is one of the reasons why he spoke up and shared with the officers that were investigating and what had to be done. And I am quite proud of the fact that he did admit to those actions that he did.

He has been in prison. It's been a positive effect on him to see what a prison has on people in his circumstances. Prison life is very difficult. And being in a protective custody unit as he is in, last week was the first time that he's had any gym time.

And, after nine months, it's very difficult being locked up for twenty-three out of twenty-four hours, not having any rehabilitation, to be in that situation, and just have gym time for the first time after nine months, and being able to get together with two or three other guys and play chess in the game room.

I'm not sure that incarceration will benefit him for a long period of time, like it hasn't for many individuals. It will give him more depression, I feel. But rehabilitation, if the correction facility can give him rehabilitation, I think that would be of exceptional benefit for him and get him on the road of recovery.

We have suggested to the court that there may be other facilities that will have a better program that will further his ability to come out of his depression and out of his difficulties. By giving him the number of years that the court has suggested, I do not believe that due to the present-day correctional institution, that that will rehabilitate him, because it hasn't, given the programs for the last nine months.

Josh's father stopped speaking. Because of Ben's sometimes convoluted syntax, Gerace felt that a moment of translation was necessary:

Judge, what I think he is trying to say also is that the time Josh is doing is particularly onerous in that he's in a cell for twenty-three hours of the day. And, when the court calculates how much time to give him, he is asking, I think, that the court bear that in mind.

And I just want to say this, Judge, that it strikes me that if Joshua is truly remorseful and is truly changing the way the thinks, the way he acts, and the way he behaves, that's great, but I have a feeling, Judge, he's either going to be a career criminal or never come back here again. I don't think there's any middle road here.

I don't know if the court gets that same sense. But there is something very odd about this entire circumstance. And I think mental-health issues are paramount. And, if the court can see its way to giving him some time, concurrent with his Meriden time, perhaps a little more, and then order a stringent mental-health regimen upon his release, I think that would go more to protecting society than lengthening his prison stay. Thank you.

The judge thanked everyone for their statements and looked out across his courtroom. "Are there any victims that are here that want to make a statement?"

Dearstyne replied, "I don't think so, but the state would like to respond to a couple of things . . ."

Dearstyne was interrupted by a voice saying that, although there were no victims in the courtroom, one victim had been in touch with the prosecutor's office and wanted to be called with the news after the sentencing hearing was complete.

Gerace said, "Joshua would like to address before the court."

The judge said, "Josh, why don't you go and then we'll have the state respond. Go ahead."

Komisarjevsky said, "Thank you, Your Honor. I just wanted to say that . . . " His voice faltered. "I'm sorry . . ."

"That's all right," the judge said. "Take your time. Take your time."

Komisarjevsky continued:

I don't know why, but I always thought that I could, that I'd be able to do everything on my own. I turned my back on my faith in God and my family. And, in doing so, I fell flat on my face and deep into hard drugs that eventually deepened my depression.

The crimes I committed were weighing so heavily on my shoulders that when the police did approach me that day, I explained to them and sat down with them and told them why and what I did, the other crimes I did and why I did them.

And the only reason I did it was because my daughter was supposed to be born within the week and I wanted a chance to start over and to start a new leaf, I guess you might say. I only pray that I have the opportunity to be able to raise my daughter in the love and the faith that now has new meaning in my life.

And I also respectfully and humbly ask if I could turn around and express my apologies in your court to my parents in front of everyone.

The judge said, "Well, I think you've already sort of done that. Okay?"

"Thank you," Komisarjevsky said.

"Is there anything else you'd like to say?"

"I am truly sorry. I wish that some of the victims had shown up today, because I really wanted to express to them that I really am sorry for the things that I did. And when I said that I wished there was more that I could do, I truly wish that there was anything that I could do more for them. I guess that's it, Your Honor."

"Anything else?" the judge said. Komisarjevsky shook his head. "All right. Does the State have anything else to add in response?"

Dearstyne said:

Quickly, and this is the obvious, I suppose, but this is not a "bite-at-the-apple" case. You've probably heard me use that term. We've used it off and on here. It's time for someone to have a "bite at the apple" and go away and do some time. It simply isn't that.

But, like I said before, his first leap into the criminal field was a huge leap, and he needs to be punished severely for that. We can discuss rehabilitation, but, quite frankly, jail time is punishment. He talks about feeling unsafe in prison and being in prison and being in a room by himself for twenty-three hours a day.

That's somewhat ironic, I suppose, because he put himself there. But, in doing that, he put other people in a sense of a prison environment also. We built walls to keep Josh or keep Mr. Komisarjevsky in prison, and now we have home-owners going out and buying alarm systems to keep people like him out.

Their fear is that someone is going to break into their home again. I've never experienced my home being broken into. Hopefully, I never will. But I will tell the court that I have had the occasion, unfortunately, to go to people's houses on several occasions to meet with them after they've come home to find their houses broken into. And I don't know if the court has any personal experience with this or not, but I know those people tend to be very distraught. It has an awful effect on your life. As far as the incidences, they didn't all happen overnight. The majority of them happened over a two-month period.

Dearstyne told the court the months and years in which each of the burglaries Komisarjevsky was charged with took place. The prosecutor pointed out that Komisarjevsky had received "special parole" in the Meriden cases and said he'd like to address the court on that subject if the judge was considering special parole in these cases.

The judge said, "All right. Well, the court is considering the special parole, and, if not for any reason but the fact that it's not clear, I don't know at this point how somebody would be supervised on both special parole and probation. The special parole program is a relatively new program. It's much more restrictive than probation. And I would not want to enter a sentence in Bristol that conflicted with the Meriden sentence. I think if he's on both special parole and probation, that might cause some problems."

Gerace said, "There was a six-year term of special parole, Judge, in Meriden."

The judge then said, "In Meriden, yes. Is there anything else that you'd want to add in terms of special parole?"

Dearstyne said:

I think the court kind of hit on my problem or my objection to special parole when you said that it's a new program. That's exactly what it is—it's a new program. And we've seen it on paper. And, at least here in Bristol, we have not seen

*it—the actual workings of it. And we've used it in the past,
mostly—we haven't used it a lot. The judges here have used
it in the past, mostly on drug cases. Judge Dunnell did use
it recently on a burglary case when she gave a young man
a period of incarceration followed by special parole. And I
objected to it for the very same reasons I'm going to object to
it today. I would submit to the court that we see it on paper
and we think we know how it's going to work, but we don't
actually know how it's going to work, because we haven't
had a chance to see it work.*

*I mean, work when someone actually gets out of jail.
Perhaps Your Honor has; I haven't. Perhaps Mr. Gerace
has. I haven't. The problem with it is this: As I understand
it—and maybe my understanding of the special parole system is wrong—the court puts Mr. Komisarjevsky on special
parole for a period of time and, hopefully, if the court's going
to do that, the court will make an order of restitution. And I
submit to the court that the way I understand special parole
is that every day you serve on special parole, that's one less
day you have to go back to jail if you fail to complete the
requirements. Am I right on that?*

The judge replied, "I think so, yes."
Gerace added, "I agree."
And so Dearstyne continued:

*So my argument in regards to that is that you put him on
special parole with a condition that he make restitution.
We're talking a large amount of money here, not an amount
that can be made in thirty days or sixty days.*

*We're talking an amount of money that has—I don't
even know if it can be made over five years, which is the*

*maximum term of probation, over five years. But we put him
on probation or on special parole for a period of time and we
tell him to make the restitution, well, every day he spends out
is one less day he goes back in. So, if we put him on special
parole for five years, with a condition that he make the restitution, what happens if he doesn't make the restitution and
it's four years before some special parole officer decides to do
something about it?*

*Now he comes back to court, and the only sentence we
can give this defendant is the year that he has left on special
parole as opposed to probation, where you have the entire
amount of the suspended time hanging over your head for
the length of the probation. I think it's fine for drug cases.
The State does not feel it's appropriate for this type of case.
A few months ago, the* [Hartford Courant] *actually had
an article on special parole and how it's being used. And
part of the argument was saying, "Well, it's new, and we
don't really know how it's going to work when people start
getting out."*

The judge said, "Well, I have a feeling that by the time
the defendant finishes his term of incarceration, whatever
the problems with special parole are might be resolved. But I
understand what your position is in terms of that."

Gerace said, "Just one more thing, Judge. If the court is
going to order restitution, I'd ask that it be reimbursed restitution. I'm sure most of these people had homeowner's
insurance."

The judge replied:

*All right. Before I begin, I would like to clarify the factors
that I'm going to consider in determining the sentence in*

these cases. The first factor that I'm going to consider is the nature and circumstances of the different offenses.

And here we have Joshua charged with, I think, fourteen cases altogether. The twelve that you pleaded guilty to all involve, I think, nighttime residential burglaries, which is probably one of the most serious crimes that somebody can commit.

Also, those crimes were committed between July 13, 2001, and February 23, 2002. And those crimes show what your operating procedure was. You would case these homes and you would commit calculated burglaries at night while people were there sleeping. You would then pawn the property and use, I guess, whatever proceeds you had to buy drugs or whatever you felt was appropriate to buy. You don't seem to be, in terms of committing burglaries, an addict just trying to get the money for a quick fix. What you do seem like is somebody who is a predator—a calculated, cold-blooded predator that decided that nighttime residential burglaries were your way to make money.

In terms of your history, it's a very unfortunate past that you've had. You've had some difficult times. It's very apparent that you have a loving family that has done as much as they can to support you, and that, unfortunately, you were subject to abuse when you were younger, and I think, for whatever reason, didn't get the treatment or counseling that you needed at that point, and that that has been a factor in your committing these crimes. But the reality of the situation is that these twelve nighttime residential burglaries are calculated crimes, intentional crimes. There is the need for the sentence to reflect the seriousness of the offenses and to promote respect for the law. As I've indicated to you, nighttime residential burglaries are probably one of the most serious crimes, because you're violating somebody's home at night, and that's when people are most vulnerable, when they're sleeping, and at least one of the cases involved a home where there were children. And, as the state indicated, a number of these people are so fearful now after having suffered what happened that they had to get alarm systems, and they feel very uncomfortable being in their own homes. So I think that really shows how serious these charges are.

In terms of the need to protect the public, which I think is another factor to take into consideration, you're a multiple offender. You now have seventeen convictions for burglary, between Bristol and Meriden. That's definitely a multiple offender. And I think it's fair to characterize your course of conduct as predatory. And I don't think that that's unfair.

In terms of the harm to the victims and the public, it's clear that the victims no longer feel safe, and many of the victims no longer feel safe in their own homes, can't sleep at night, needed to install alarm systems in a number of cases.

I need to determine what's necessary to provide just punishment. I need to determine what's necessary to protect the public by isolating you from society for some period of time. I also have to consider the goal of specific deterrence, to make sure that you understand that once you're released from custody, you cannot commit these crimes any longer, and that there are going to be consequences if you do so. And I also need to impose a sentence that reflects the goal of general deterrence—that other people will be warned that if they commit similar crimes, there are going to be serious consequences for those crimes.

Now, in determining what the final sentence is going to be, the court believes that it needs to impose a sentence that does not conflict with the Meriden sentence. The Meriden sentence—the total effective sentence in Meriden is three *years in the custody of the commissioner of correction, six years special parole. As we've indicated, special parole is a new program. It's supposed to be much more restrictive than probation. I think it would cause problems in this case having you on both probation and special parole. For those reasons, I think that special parole is appropriate, not only because I think you need that heightened level of supervision that special parole can provide, but also to make sure that the sentence does not conflict with the Meriden sentence. I need to sentence you on twelve cases.*

The judge went through the charges, case by case, and determined the punishment for each. When he was done, he tallied the score.

So the total effective sentence is nine years' imprisonment in the custody of the commissioner of correction, six years' special parole. And that sentence is to run concurrent to the Meriden sentence. So what that means is for the next fifteen years of your life, from twenty-two to thirty-seven, you're going to be either incarcerated or on special parole. So, if you can't change your life around in the next seventeen years, there's really no hope for you. I would hope that you would take to heart and hope that you were sincere when you indicated that you've come to resolve that you might be doing a lot of time. Don't waste that time. Use it to better yourself.

Also, as conditions of special parole, you will undergo a substance-abuse evaluation and mental-health evaluation, and comply with any treatment as deemed appropriate, including random screening. Take all meds as prescribed. Pay all restitution within the period of the six years of special parole. You must obtain full-time, verifiable employment or be attending school full-time. You must also pay child support. For the restitution, it's for any lost or damaged property, unreimbursed, verified. You will have no contact with any of the victims or their dwellings.

The judge signed the necessary papers and the hearing was concluded.

While in prison Komisarjevsky wrote letters to a female friend on the outside talking about how he really wanted to go straight, maybe take up a career in real estate. He just hoped he had the strength to do it, that the "criminal demon" inside of him didn't take over again.

According to Bill Glass, a retired local cop who'd known Komisarjevsky for years, Joshua had nasty habits other than just being a burglar. There were indications that he had sexual issues as well. "He terrorized my older daughter's best friend from the time she was probably in seventh or eighth grade right through high school. He'd be peeking in her windows. There were two burglaries at her house. Not just valuable items were stolen, but lingerie-type items as well. At the time we didn't suspect him, but later on we did find out that he did do it."

Komisarjevsky served half of his sentence before being released to a halfway house, the Berman Treatment Center at 140 Sargeant Street in Hartford, on June 6, 2006. Berman, according to the Connecticut Department of Correction, was a seventeen-bed "intensive in-patient substance abuse treatment program" where "all clients receive urine/breathalyzer monitoring, education and therapy groups, individual and group counseling, pre-release/life skills training, employment readiness, anger management, and participation in community service projects. Upon completion, clients are often referred to the work release residential programs."

Komisarjevsky lived in the halfway house for several months, and it was there that he met Hayes. In fact, the two were roommates for about a week at Berman during the summer of 2006. According to an official at the Berman House, the pair both completed a five-week substance-abuse program while there. They were later transferred to another facility called the Silliman House, a twenty-four-bed work release facility, where they continued to share a room for as long as four months. The Silliman House was on Retreat Avenue in Hartford, next door to Hartford Hospital. In order to stay at the Silliman House, an ex-con had to be sixteen or older and had to be referred by the Department of Correction. This domestic situation lasted for Hayes and Komisarjevsky until Hayes was kicked out of the Silliman House for drug use and sent to the J.B. Gates Correctional Institution in Niantic.

According to Terri Saiya, spokeswoman for Community Solutions Inc., which ran both the Berman and Silliman facilities, "The men may very well have had what you'd consider normal interactions. Our clients eat together, attend groups together, and certainly have opportunities to interact. But if any of our staff had any reason to believe there was an inappropriate relationship of any kind it would have been reported and handled internally, and there is absolutely no indication of that."

Though one was young and the other middle-aged, and they had almost humorously variant builds, the two got along right away. They had things in common. They were both burglars. They were both fathers. Komisarjevsky told Hayes that he had a daughter who was five, and that he'd been in jail when she was born. Hayes told Komisarjevsky that he was the father of two teenagers who lived with their mother and stepfather in the town of Torrington. Somewhere along the line they decided they would make a pretty good team on the outside.

After being released from prison, Komisarjevsky became embroiled in a nasty custody battle with his ex-girlfriend over custody of their daughter Jayda. He was awarded full custody of the five-year-old child one month before the Petit murders. Jayda then came to live with the Komisarjevskys.

Friends of the Komisarjevsky family told reporters that the family was "devastated" by Joshua's involvement in the Petit murders. One friend, who did not wish to be identified, said, "Joshua was a troubled child, and most of the family had little or no contact with him. Ben and Jude are very hard-working people. They did everything they could bringing him up. When you have a teenager who robs and goes to jail, it's tragic."

William Gerace, Komisarjevsky's attorney back in 2002, said that Joshua had always struck him as a shy, withdrawn, polite type, who, back then, seemed genuinely contrite.

"I have trouble squaring the young man I knew with the heinous crimes against the Petit family," Gerace said. "His pregnant girlfriend would come to court like clockwork. She was very worried about him not being able to see the baby if he did time."

When Joshua was released on parole from the halfway house in 2007, he was ordered to wear an electronic ankle bracelet for ninety days so that authorities could make sure he stayed home at night. He got a job with the Hartford Restorative Services, a roofing and masonry company with offices in Glastonbury.

Komisarjevsky must have really been counting the days until the ankle bracelet came off on July 19, 2007. Three days later he and Steven Hayes broke into their first house together. One day after that, they broke into the Petit home.

Police researched the background of Steven Hayes and learned that he had been born in Florida, raised by a single mother. At the time of his arrest, he still lived with his mother in the working-class Connecticut town of Winsted, population 7,000, which was about thirty miles away from Cheshire.

Steven had a brother, Brian, and their dad had left home when both were small children. Neighbors used to complain about the loud and seemingly violent fights that broke out frequently between the fatherless siblings.

Hayes, like Komisarjevsky, had been a burglar for most of his life. He had been in and out of prison ever since he was a kid. But, while Komisarjevsky's specialty was the nighttime invasion of houses, Hayes usually broke into cars. Whereas Komisarjevsky had used technology in his escapades, Hayes was a brute-force type of guy.

Sometimes he stole the car itself, if he needed wheels to get someplace, but most often he stole and sold any electronics he could find. He didn't have a fancy way of breaking into the automobiles. Usually he picked up a big rock and used it to smash open a window.

Hayes first entered the criminal system on June 30, 1980. During that decade he was a resident of both the ironically named Manson Youth Institution and the Cheshire Correctional Institution. Between his first arrest when he was a kid and his final crimes in 2007, Hayes did time at *seventeen* different prisons and detention centers. Between his first incarceration in 1980 and the Petit murders, Hayes racked up twenty-three disciplinary tickets, including busts for public intoxication and fighting.

As often happens with career criminals, Hayes became so accustomed to prison living that he existed more easily inside than outside. According to one Winsted neighbor who did not want to be identified, "When he got out of jail, he didn't know how to live in the real world."

On October 1, 2003, Hayes began serving a five-year sentence for breaking into a car and stealing a purse. He had served three years of that sentence when he was granted parole during May 2006 and released on June 13, 2006, to a halfway house. It was while living in the halfway house that Hayes met Komisarjevsky. But he subsequently was reincarcerated for a drug-use violation on November 26, 2006, and was given seven more months behind bars. By May of 2007, he was again back on the street.

Now, as investigators interrogated Hayes regarding the Petit murders, they learned what many had known before. He didn't come off as a hardened criminal. He didn't seem tough, or evil, or rebellious, or any of that. Hayes had a very mild personality.

During their long criminal careers, only Komisarjevsky had displayed harbingers of what was to come. In 2002 a judge had realized that Komisarjevsky was a "predator" who needed to be punished. And yet, during the summer of 2007, he was free among us and raring to start up right where he'd left off before his last arrest. Hayes, on the other hand, although he'd been in the system longer, had remained comparatively inconspicuous. A middle-aged man who'd been in most of the jails and prisons in the area, he was still viewed by the law as a run-of-the-mill junkie, not someone to be punished at all. Someone to be cured. Well, if there ever was a chance to "cure" Steven Hayes, it died on the day he found himself rooming with Joshua Komisarjevsky. Hayes and Komisarjevsky were two halves of a whole, and together they were far more dangerous than either could be alone. Their two heads, when placed together, formed something that could only be described as evil.

Chapter 6:

"We Plan to Seek the Death Penalty"

On Thursday, July 26, 2007, the Petit family released a written statement that read:

We are a family of faith. No one ever wants their faith tested, particularly by events such as these. When there is no ability to control your life events and you are required to deal with such great tragedy and loss, however, your faith is all the more necessary. Although we will no longer have Jennifer, Hayley, and Michaela physically present with us, and we do now and we will continue to experience an extraordinary sense of loss because of that, we firmly believe that their spirits and all of the goodness that defined their characters and beautiful personas will remain with us forever. We are committed to preserving those spirits and fulfilling their lives of promise, so tragically cut short.

Many ask what they can do. Care about others as a regular part of your lives, not just at times of tragedy. The feelings of connectedness and the outpouring of affection for us and our family members represent the best of human emotions, for which we are extremely grateful. Actively support causes that exist solely for the improvement of people's lives in need. Doing these things will be your way of saying that these senseless acts of violence did not stop the wonderful, giving spirits of our beloved family members. . . . We thank you all for your prayers, expressions of sympathy, and interest in doing something positive in response to this awful tragedy.

On the same day that the grieving family released that statement, the suspects were charged. According to New Haven
Superior Court documents, Komisarjevsky and Hayes were
charged with:

One count:
First-degree assault (of William Petit)
First-degree aggravated sexual assault (of Hawke-Petit for
    Hayes, unspecified for Komisarjevsky)
First-degree burglary
First-degree arson
First-degree conspiracy to commit arson
First-degree robbery
First-degree larceny
Two counts:
Risk of injury to a minor
Six counts: capital felony
Murder of two or more persons at the same time and in the
    course of a single transaction
Murder of a person under sixteen (Michaela)
Murder of a kidnapped person (Hawke-Petit)
Murder of a kidnapped person (Hayley)
Murder of a kidnapped person (Michaela)
Murder of a person during a first-degree sexual assault
Six counts: First-degree kidnapping
Kidnapping of Michaela
Kidnapping of Hayley
Kidnapping of Hawke-Petit (with intention to compel third
    person to pay or deliver money or property as ransom)
Kidnapping of Hawke-Petit (restrained the person and
    abducted with the intent to accomplish or advance the
    commission of a felony)

Kidnapping of Hawke-Petit (restrained the person and
abducted with intent to terrorize her or a third person)
Kidnapping of William Petit

No one was surprised when Michael Dearington, the State's attorney for the judicial district of New Haven, announced that he planned to seek the death penalty against both men. "In more than twenty-five years as a prosecutor, I have sought the death penalty only once," Dearington said, referring to a 2000 case in which a man fatally stabbed his aunt and two cousins. In that case, Dearington refused to make a deal in which the defendant would plead guilty in exchange for life in prison without chance of parole. Eventually, life was the sentence anyway, after the defendant presented evidence of a troubled childhood. "This week, I did it twice," Dearington continued. "I thought it was important with respect to the family, the public, and law enforcement. I seek capital charges when they are warranted. It's as simple as that."

The statement elicited immediate protests from groups opposed to the death penalty. Robert Nave, the director of the Connecticut Network to Abolish the Death Penalty, posted a statement on the group's website, saying, "We have seen over and over that the pursuit and imposition of the death penalty only perpetuates the suffering of survivors, makes celebrities out of murderers, and costs the taxpayers far more than if life without release is sought."

New Haven public defender Thomas Ullman said that his office, to avoid a conflict of interest, could only represent one of the defendants. The state would have to appoint lawyers with capital case experience to defend the other. "We will fight the death penalty charges tooth and nail," Ullman said.

The state's attorney in Waterbury, John A. Connelly, didn't see any way that his colleague, Michael Dearington, could avoid seeking the death penalty in this case. "This case is the most horrendous murder in this state in the last thirty years. There are about five ways you could charge capital felony," Connelly said. According to Connecticut law, capital murder charges can be brought for intentionally causing the death of someone under sixteen; of two or more people in the same incident; or of someone during a sexual assault or kidnapping. The criteria had been met across the board.

Another factor in seeking the death penalty in a case is the amount of publicity the case has received. "It doesn't get any more high-profile than this," said Connelly. "I think the public is demanding justice on this one."

When hearing of Connelly's statement, Ullman responded, "He is polluting the jury pool and violated a code of professional ethics." Connelly, in turn, responded, "I was simply answering questions posed by a reporter, and I was answering them correctly."

Even if convicted and sentenced to death, there was a question as to whether or not the accused would ever actually be executed. At that time there were seven inmates on Connecticut's death row, but the state had executed only one prisoner in the last forty-seven years—that being serial killer Michael Bruce Ross, who was executed on May 13, 2005.

As the murders continued to dominate the news throughout New England, WCVB-TV in Boston was reporting that gun sales in central Connecticut were through the roof. Scott Hoffman, the owner of Hoffman's Gun Center on the Berlin Turnpike in nearby Newington, Connecticut, said, "People are rushing to the store to buy guns for themselves and their homes. They are lining up to take gun-safety classes so they can buy firearms. They're scared—scared for their own personal safety and their family's safety, their children's safety, and they want a way to protect themselves. You talk to these people and you can see it has hit home, this particular crime. It is the sheer grotesqueness of the crime and the fact that it's such a normal family. The most popular weapon for both men and women looking to defend themselves is the defense-grade shotgun. Part of the reason for that popularity is the short waiting time. It can be obtained in two weeks as opposed to waiting ninety days for a pistol permit. We sell about 8,000 guns per year, and I'd say the majority of them are for self-defense."

Sales of home-security systems also increased dramatically in the days immediately following the Cheshire murders. According to Joe Mitchell of Associated Security Corp., the phones had been ringing off the hook. Mitchell said, "Security systems used to be purchased by people who were looking to protect their valuables, but no more. Today many people are getting them to protect their lives."

The murders had been so horrifying that, for a few days, they were on the national news just as much as the local news. A national sense of insecurity was experienced, a sense of universal nervousness that hadn't been so strong since the 1969 Manson murders. In reaction to this sense of insecurity, *ABC News* broadcast, and placed on its website, recommendations for homeowners who wanted to feel more secure. These recommendations included:

1. If you have children, put two peepholes in your front door, one high and one low. "People, especially children, are less likely to open the door if they can see who is on the other side."
2. Home alarms are good, but know that for experienced criminals they are not that hard to bypass. "Still, security signs have been known to put off burglars."
3. Your alarm should make a loud noise, loud enough to waken everyone and frighten the burglar.
4. Secure your windows. "When home invaders break into windows, it is usually because they are unlocked, especially bathroom windows."
5. Hang chimes in the window area. Put plants that have thorns on them outside the house.
6. If you are not in a safe place, they can get to you. Turn a closet into a safe room. Put a deadbolt lock on the closet door. Put a light source inside the closet and keep a cell phone inside.
7. Write a list of emergency numbers on the back of the door so that you've got them in case of panic.
8. Always call 911.
9. Keep your house lit, even when you are away.
10. Cut the trees and bushes around your house low, so they do not provide potential intruders with a place to hide.

Back on Sorghum Mill Drive, people were having a lot of trouble sleeping at night. Folks woke up hourly and checked to make sure the doors were locked.

Deborah Raducha, a past president of the Deaconwood neighborhood's homeowners' association, said, "This is a neighborhood terrorized. They should add terrorizing a neighborhood to the list of things they've arrested those thugs for. This is the reason I left New Britain. I woke up at three a.m. today scared to death. And what's really offensive is that someone was leaving flyers in everyone's mailboxes today about a security system. Talk about taking advantage of a horrible situation."

The troubled sleep didn't go away. As late as that winter, although months had passed since the Petit murders, Cheshire and its neighboring towns in central Connecticut were still feeling the effects. Insecurity. Anxiety. Fear. Insomnia. Trauma is like that.

With that in mind, on Tuesday, February 26, 2008, the Seymour Land Trust and Police Department held a seminar to help residents learn how to avoid becoming a victim of a crime. About sixty people attended.

"People who are going to commit crimes are going to do it," said Community Police Officer Joe DeFelice. "You have got to be prepared. There are simple things people can do, such as locking doors. Many people grew up in a society where they didn't lock their doors. I can't tell you how many calls I get where the people say, 'I never lock my doors.' Lock your doors.

"Criminals usually aren't fancy. The tools they use are cheap and easy to get. A burglar with a crowbar can easily lift a sliding glass door off its track. It is very easy to do. To prevent that, you have to install quality deadbolts and use them properly. A lot of times, people will leave a key inside in the deadbolt. That doesn't make a lot of sense."

Another thing that homeowners did that only encouraged crime was to leave keys outside a door. Officer DeFelice said,

"I can't tell you how many homes I've gone to where there's a fake rock by the door. They are plastic rocks designed to hold keys, and they are supposed to blend in with the landscaping. A burglar with a trained eye can pick out the fake rock right away, and that makes it just so easy for someone to get into your home."

Lieutenant Paul Satkowski also spoke to the gathering, saying that it was not a good idea to keep a handgun inside the house for protection.

"Many feel that firearms are the way to protect themselves. We disagree," he said. "As police officers, we often come across people carrying guns, so they are a threat to the safety of the police as well. Guns in the home are twenty-two times more likely to be used for something other than self-defense."

It was a sobering stat.

"We recommend you be a good witness and call the police," he said. "All too often people take the law into their own hands and get themselves into a jam."

None of this was intended to imply that homeowners did not have the right to bear arms. It was a right guaranteed by the U.S. Constitution and shored up by the Connecticut "Castle Act," which says that a man's home is his castle. Homeowners are allowed to use a "reasonable force" to protect their property. They are not, however, allowed to use deadly force unless they believe that their own lives are in danger. This interpretation of the law is to prevent people from shooting trespassers who are walking across their lawns.

"Deadly force can't be used unless one believes the attacker is going to use deadly force or inflict great physical harm. Deadly force can't be used if one can safely retreat from the situation," Lieutenant Satkowski concluded.

As far as Satkowski was concerned, he couldn't repeat the "deadly force" rule often enough. With the climate of fear that existed in central Connecticut, everyone would be lucky if there were no tragic accidents. It was a "shoot first, ask questions later" mood, and that kind of thinking often led to disaster.

Chapter 7:

Services—Private and Public

Dr. Petit was released from St. Mary's Hospital on Friday morning, July 27, so that he could bury his family. The first order of business when he was released was a visit from a tailor. He had to be measured for a suit. All of his clothes had been destroyed in the fire.

While Dr. Petit was still hospitalized, family members made funeral arrangements through the Bailey Funeral Home. As soon as Dr. Petit was well enough to leave the hospital, they held a private funeral for his wife and two daughters.

The services were held at the family's church, the Cheshire United Methodist Church. Jennifer, Hayley, and Michaela were then buried in a cemetery in Plainville. The exact location of the burial was kept private to avoid a rush of curiosity seekers.

The Bailey Funeral Home posted obituaries for the Petits online. Jennifer's obit noted that her middle name was Lynn and she had been born in Morristown, New Jersey, on September 26, 1958, the daughter of Reverend Richard and Marybelle Hawke. She had graduated from Greenville Senior High School in Pennsylvania, and earned a degree in nursing from Sharon School of Nursing in Sharon, Pennsylvania. The obituary read:

> *Jennifer's loving and generous nature carried through her career as a Pediatric Oncology Nurse at the Children's Hospital of Pittsburgh where she would meet the love of her life, Bill. Prior to marriage, she was employed in Rochester, New York, as a Pediatric Nurse at the Strong Memorial Hospital.*

Jen and Bill were married on April 13, 1985, in Meadville, Pennsylvania, and continued their medical careers together at Yale–New Haven Hospital. They grew in faith together at Cheshire United Methodist Church, where Jennifer served on numerous committees there. Their family was complete with the joyous births of her two daughters, Hayley Elizabeth and Michaela Rose.

Hayley's obit gave her birth date, October 15, 1989, and noted that she was a June graduate of Miss Porter's School, "where she was well loved and admired as a student, athlete, a leader and friend." Her academic achievements came next: honor roll, *cum laude*, journalism prize-winner, early admission to Dartmouth. Then athletics: three-season varsity player of cross-country, basketball, and crew; a two-season varsity captain of basketball and crew; and her election to the all-school senior leadership position of athletic association head. "Hayley's leadership and dedication led her to be the winner of her high school's award for 'exceptional community service.' She started 'Hayley's Hope,' raising thousands of dollars in support of multiple sclerosis research," the obit concluded.

The final obituary read:

Michaela came into the world smiling on November 17, 1995. She was looking forward to attending middle school at Chase Collegiate for the upcoming school year. As Hayley went to college, she planned to carry on the work her sister had started with "Hayley's Hope" and renaming it "Michaela's Miracle." Michaela enjoyed sports and attended the summer "Athletic Experience" at Miss Porter's School in

Farmington, playing soccer, basketball, and lacrosse. Picking up her love of music from her mother, she recently had her first flute solo at the Cheshire United Methodist Church. Michaela's perpetual smile will forever be remembered and missed by everyone.

The triple obit also noted that:

The sisters are survived by their father, William A. Petit Jr., M.D.; their paternal grandparents, William and Barbara Petit, Plainville, Conn.; their maternal grandparents, Richard and Marybelle Hawke, Slippery Rock and Venice, Fla.; their maternal great-grandmother, Florence Triano; their Aunt Cindy and Uncle Bill Renn and their children, Evan and Lydia; Uncle Glenn Petit and his children, Rachel and Alicia, and their children, Jacob and Molly; Aunt Kyla; Uncle Mike and Aunt Erin Petit and their children, Michael, Brooke, Tristan and Paige; Uncle Brian Petit; and Aunt Johanna and Uncle Dennis Chapman and their children, Abby and Andrew. They also leave their great-aunts and -uncles, Jean McNuff, Judith Hodge, Jim Buchanan, Elnora Richards, John Hawke, Johanna and Joseph Ierna, Frank Triano, Andrea and James LaChapelle, Edward and Roberta Petit, Beverly and Larry Joyce, Sharon and Eugene Beaulieu, Gary Petit, and Clara, Marilyn, Victoria, Sally and Linda Petit; and many dear friends.

There followed various addresses for mourners to send contributions. [Those addresses and others can be found in the appendix to this book.]

As the private funeral service was under way, a search warrant request was being drawn up by detectives Canon and

Vitello for legal permission to search and seize evidence from the red pickup truck driven by Hayes on the night of the murders, which had been found in the parking lot at the Maplecroft Plaza. The search warrant request specified the vehicle by Connecticut registration number and vehicle identification number, stating that it was a 2003 red Sierra pickup. The warrant sought permission to use a K-9 team trained in the detection of accelerants to search the vehicle for flammable liquids, volatile substances, incendiary devices, and containers that could hold those substances. The request noted that the vehicle had already been seized by the police and was, at that point, located at the Connecticut State Barracks in Bethany.

According to the request:

On Monday, July 23, 2007, at approximately 1500 hours, Detective Matthew Gunsalus of the Connecticut State Police Central Crime Unit located the red pickup truck [redacted] at the Stop & Shop Plaza on Highland Avenue. An NCIC check . . . identified the registered owner to be Philip Theeb Jr., of Torrington, Connecticut. The vehicle was seized and transported to the State Police Barracks. . . . On Tuesday, July 24, 2007, at approximately 1402 hours, detectives Gunsalus and [Francis] Budwitz of the Connecticut State Police Major Crime Unit met with Philip Theeb and obtained a consent to search the . . . pickup. On Wednesday, July 25, 2007, between the hours of 1500 and 1930, members of the Police Major Crime Squad processed the vehicle for any and all items of evidentiary value. During the course of the processing, a purple knapsack with the initials "HEP" embroidered on it was located on the front passenger floor that contains clothes, loose change (large amount), a wallet for William Petit containing an ID and credit cards, and a

*wallet for Jennifer Hawke-Petit containing an ID and credit
cards. Also located on the front passenger floor was a plastic
CVS bag containing two (2) pearl necklaces. It is unknown
to investigators when these items were placed in the truck.
Located on the left exterior edge of the driver's seat is an
area with a red blood-like stain that is believed to be blood.
Located underneath the cup holder that is built into the center console was a wallet for Steven Hayes containing operator's license and miscellaneous cards.*

The family knew that public services for their three lost loved
ones were going to draw a crowd, so they obtained permission
to hold the services inside the 1,850-seat Welte Hall on the Central Connecticut State University campus. As it turned out, this
auditorium was not large enough.

The services were held at 11:00 a.m. on Saturday. More
than 3,000 people showed up. A side location was set up, with
speakers, so the overflow crowd could hear. The stage at the
front of the auditorium was adorned with flowers, and there
were three large photos of Jennifer, Hayley, and Michaela.

Some of Hayley's classmates from Miss Porter's School
spoke. Then colleagues of Jennifer's at Cheshire Academy had
their turn. Relatives took turns speaking, battling their emotions as they remembered and read passages from the Bible.

"We hope that being together will not be in vain, but will
bring about a strength to all of us," said Ms. Hawke-Petit's
father, the Reverend Richard Hawke, who then led the audi-
ence in a prayer.

"This is the second hardest thing I've ever done in my life.
The hardest thing came yesterday when we buried Jen, Hayley,
and Michaela. The hole left in our hearts is deep and wide," said

Johanna Chapman, Dr. Petit's sister. "Losing Michaela at age eleven is possibly the greatest loss of all, because she never got the chance to show us just how great she could have been."

About Hayley, Johanna said, "I'll never forget how inquisitive she was when she was a little girl, always asking tough questions, like, 'How was the universe formed?' She was the big cousin that all of her other cousins looked up to. The short time Hayley was here, what a difference she made. Can you imagine what she could have done?" Those last words were choked with sobs.

The featured speaker, of course, was Dr. Petit. The poor man. People burst into tears at the very thought of this man's predicament. How could he go on? How could he exist knowing what had happened—all of the things that had been taken away that could never be given back.

Not everyone in the crowd really knew the man personally. But they probably knew his story and knew that, in the medical world, he was a big deal. Although Dr. Petit lived in Cheshire, his practice was in the neighboring town of Plainville. He was a member of the Plainville Chamber of Commerce. He had grown up and lived his entire life in the central Connecticut area.

He was the son of a store owner. His father, William A. Petit Sr., used to sell trinkets in a small store on Plainville's Whiting Street, twelve miles to the north of Cheshire. The elder William still lived in Plainville. When the younger William began practicing medicine, he set up his office just a few blocks away from the home he'd grown up in. The walls of his office were covered with photos of his family.

He met Jennifer Hawke, the woman he was to marry, at Children's Hospital in Pittsburgh. He was a third-year medical student and she was a new nurse. They met in a patient's room in the children's hospital. Dr. Petit even remembered the patient. Her name was Becky, and she had a kidney problem.

Jennifer was musical, and played both the guitar and the piano. On their first date they went out to dinner with his parents and two of his parents' friends. They were married in April 1985. Dr. Petit and his family had lived in the house at 300 Sorghum Mill Drive since 1989.

Now, in this auditorium, Dr. Petit was the focus of all attention. Though he was obviously wounded during the murder of his family—a visible scar remained from his attack, a vertical line on his forehead above his right eyebrow—he also seemed intact. Stalwart. His voice was firm and collected as he thanked everyone for coming, the authorities, and the choir that had performed. Then, one by one, he talked about the loved ones he had lost.

First, Jennifer. Petit said that his wife had graduated in 1976 from Greenville High School in Pennsylvania. She attended nursing school and still worked in the medical field, as the health-center director at Cheshire Academy, and was an active member of the family's church, Cheshire United Methodist Church, where she had taught Sunday school.

He recalled the relationship between his wife and his daughters: "They were really more like sisters. I had to keep saying to her, 'You're their mother, not their sister.' Still, she knew more about how to take care of kids than I ever would."

Then he talked about Hayley, how she'd had sharp basketball skills from the time she was ten, and how she'd become involved, through Hayley's Hope, with raising money for the Multiple Sclerosis Society's Greater Connecticut Chapter. For eight years she had been raising money—the eight years since she'd learned her mother was suffering from the disease.

"It was really Hayley of her own accord," said Dr. Petit. "She thought her mom was going to die, and she figured if she did something, she could save her." The team Hayley put together organized an annual walk that had collected more than $50,000 to help combat MS.

He noted that Hayley had graduated from Miss Porter's School and had been accepted to go to his alma mater, Dartmouth, in the fall, and described how proud he was that the essay she wrote for her application was called "My Dad." Dr. Petit read a portion of Hayley's essay:

> *My dad looked on as my four-year-old hands clasped the handle of the black medical bag he had given to me on my fourth birthday. Looking inside, I saw a child's stethoscope and various other instruments which mirrored his professional tools. From then on, I had gone with my dad to the hospital on Saturdays. I loved trailing behind Dad's long white coattails through the endless maze of hallways with shiny white floors. I was always fascinated when he strode confidently into a patient's room, talked to them for a few minutes and recommended a treatment. I clearly remember how he always made the patients laugh or smile before leaving. He possesses this amazing God-like power, not only to heal people physically, but also to make them feel safe and brighten their days. His presence made the hospital seem a fortress and anyone within its walls safe.*

When he spoke about Michaela, he remembered coming home after a long day at work and finding her in front of the television set, watching the Food Network, her attention fixed. He remembered that she was a vegetarian and how she loved to cook.

"I knew that if I wanted to watch the basketball game, I was going to have to catch it in my office upstairs," he said. "Only when it was a particularly long day would I pull rank."

He recalled that Michaela had inherited her mother's musical talent and had recently performed her first flute solo in church, and how she had a shy way of greeting people, sometimes staring at the carpet. But once she knew you, she had no trouble looking you straight in the eye and flashing that smile of hers.

"Once you had the smile, you knew you were in," he said. "For an eleven-year-old, her iPod became filled with the Beatles, Elton John, the Police, and the Beach Boys. I think she had more Beach Boys songs than anybody. She would hear a song once in the car and know it and be able to sing it on key."

She played basketball with her dad just as Hayley had, but she didn't like to go to UConn games. She was bored. Petit said, "I told her this was going to be the big year, and I said, 'You know, time is up. Hayley's going off to college and you're going to have to go to the UConn games with me. You're going to have to learn how to do your homework in the car like Haze did.'

"She had an innate sense of fairness that I didn't know but heard about from her teachers that she would always stick up for the kids in the class if a kid was excluded," Petit said. "Maybe it was that that made her stick up for the kids that were being picked on." The father choked back tears as he said, "She was a wonderful, wonderful little girl who was going to grow up to be a beautiful woman."

He recalled how he felt lying in his bed at St. Mary's Hospital in Waterbury. His first instinct, he admitted, was to hide and not face things. But that wasn't the way Petits did things. They went out and worked, worked for the common good.

He concluded by saying, "I guess if there's anything to be gained from the senseless deaths of my beautiful family, it's for us all to go forward with the inclination to *live with a faith that embodies action*. Help a neighbor, fight for a cause, love your family. I'm really expecting all of you to go out and do some of these things with your family, in your own little way, to spread the work of these three wonderful women. Thank you."

The twenty-minute speech was stunningly inspiring. How could he do it? How could a man in such emotional distress hold himself together like that? People were amazed. The crowd had gathered to help comfort this man and came away, instead, feeling comforted by him. What's more, his speech was a *call to action*. His family wasn't around to do service for the community and the world anymore, so it was up to those gathered here to *do it for them*. He had, in essence, created an army of thousands to carry out the work of his wife and daughters—and they couldn't wait to get started.

Among those who attended the service was seventeen-year-old Megan Alexander, who had been a friend of Hayley's since third grade. She had gone to grammar school at Chase Collegiate with Hayley and high school at Cheshire Academy, where Jennifer worked. So there had always been a Petit around.

Megan recalled, "I was leaving the memorial with four other girls who had gone to Cheshire Academy, and we were talking to a *60 Minutes* producer to set up a time to meet, and he looked at us and said, 'You're about to be mobbed by the nation.' I hadn't been looking around, and when I looked up, there was a wall of reporters and photographers. It was chaos. We were all seventeen at the time, and none of us were with our parents. We ended up standing outside the auditorium for over an hour just crushed by reporters."

She told one reporter that Jennifer Hawke-Petit, "Jen" as she called her, was like a second mom to the girls who attended the academy, many of whom were boarders and came from other countries. "She was always there for you," Megan said of Hayley's mom.

For a time she talked to a reporter from the *New York Post*. One of the questions he asked her was whether she knew the murderers. "I know that one guy is from my town, but I don't recognize him," she said. Having read the papers, she knew Komisarjevsky lived in Cheshire.

When the *New York Post* came out the next day, Megan was quoted as saying, "We all recognized him. He used to mow lawns all over Cheshire." Steamed, Megan called the reporter to complain. "We went back and forth a few times," she later explained. "I said, 'I didn't say that.' He said, 'Yes you did. I wrote it down.' So I was like, whatever, there's not going to be a lawsuit over this or anything, so I let it go.

"After everything happened, everyone started talking, and there *was* a lot of speculation about how this guy could have become associated with the family," Megan continued. "And one of my friends who is a landscaper said he might have seen him mowing lawns. But I don't know. I never saw him mowing a lawn. I never saw the guy."

Outside the auditorium after the public services, Megan wasn't the only one dealing with the tsunami of press. Asked for memories, Megan's mom, Deb Hereld, told of Hayley's graduation party, but the thing she remembered most was Michaela, how she skipped around happily and turned to flash her a smile.

Plainville Town Councilman Christopher J. Wazorko said, "I always kind of joked, if you weren't with your own family, you'd certainly want to be a Petit."

"As much as we weep, as much as we mourn their loss, as much as we miss them, God weeps with us," said the Petits' pastor, Reverend Stephen Volpe.

Following the public memorial, the Petit family released another statement to the public online:

> *We want to extend our sincere thanks to the Connecticut State Police, the Cheshire Police Department, the Plainville Police Department, and all of the other local police and fire departments who worked together yesterday to allow our families and friends the opportunity to provide our beloved girls a beautiful and reverent church tribute and a quiet cemetery service where we were able to grieve, console, and say our good-byes in private. The Cheshire United Methodist Church community has been an important part of Jennifer and Bill's family life for many years—never more important than yesterday. We will be forever grateful for the love and concern of Reverend Volpe, the members of the wonderful choir and music program, and all of the members of the congregation for their special efforts to make yesterday's service so meaningful to us all.*
>
> *As the funeral procession made its way from Plainville to Cheshire and back again, our hearts were touched by the many people who stood at the side of the road with hands over their hearts and tears flowing from their eyes. We were also moved by signs along the route expressing sympathy for our family and the loss we have suffered. We are very much aware that our grief is shared by many of you, and we are thankful for your prayers and support.*

Jennifer's father, Reverend Richard Hawke, observed that people sometimes question how God can allow such tragic events to occur, but assured us that God is not in any way responsible for this awful tragedy; to the contrary, he said, God is crying with us.

There is no way to adequately state the importance of the need to properly grieve and recognize the wonderful lives of loved ones suddenly and violently removed from you. We are grateful for the members of the media who have respected our wishes and allowed us to deal with our grief privately.

We thank the administration and personnel at Central Connecticut State University, the Hospital of Central Connecticut, and the Hartford County Medical Association for all they have done for today's memorial service at Welte Auditorium. Their generosity enables us to accommodate the many friends, schoolmates, co-workers, and patients who also want the opportunity to pay proper tribute to Jennifer, Hayley, and Michaela.

As Bill has challenged us, it is now up to all of us to go forward together to carry out the legacy that Jennifer, Hayley, and Michaela so beautifully began: to care about one another, to work to advance an important cause, and to recognize that each of us has the opportunity and the power to make our community and our society a better place to live. Thank you again for all of your support. God bless you all.

It wasn't just central Connecticut that mourned. In Greenville, Pennsylvania—a town only a quarter of the size of Cheshire—where Jennifer had grown up, a memorial was held with more than forty of her old friends and classmates attending. They remembered her as the class treasurer, a member of the Bios Club, and a member of the homecoming court.

Among those in attendance was Jennifer's hometown friend, Joy Miller, who said she couldn't have been more shocked when she heard the news about her old friend. "You don't expect that to happen to someone you know, someone from Greenville."

Also there was Reverend Pamela Gardner, the pastor at Slippery Rock United Methodist Church, which Jennifer's mother and father attended during the summer. When Jennifer's father retired, he and Marybelle moved to Venice, Florida, but still spent their summers in western Pennsylvania. Gardner said, "Dick is very devastated. Marybelle is keeping herself busy. But there is no malice in their hearts toward whomever did this." The pastor said that upon hearing the news, the Hawkes had flown to Connecticut in a private jet that a concerned millionaire offered them.

In the meantime, in Pittsburgh, where Dr. Petit had attended medical school, the news made old friends cry. One old friend, Marcy Edington, now a nurse practitioner in Upper St. Clair, reminisced about the old days.

"I remember a group of UPMC [University of Pittsburgh Medical Center] Montefiore nurses would meet up with Dr. Petit and some friends for drinks at Zelda's Greenhouse in Oakland. It's closed now. I heard the news when they showed the picture on *Good Morning America*. It's such a tragedy, just so random. The wickedness of the world can be just so random," she said.

Megan Alexander may not have seen Komisarjevsky around, but there were residents who remembered the local who had suddenly become one of the nation's most notorious murderers. One was Julianne Clayton (a pseudonym), a lifelong townie who had returned to Cheshire after college. She was the same age as Josh and had met him when they both were about thirteen.

"He 'went out' with a friend of mine," Julianne recalled. "Normally, I would have long forgotten any of my friends' brief romances—especially those that happened, what, twelve, thirteen years ago—but I remember this one for one reason only: his last name. My friend and I would try to spell his name over and over again while at her house after school. She was crazy about him, and for good reason: Josh was pretty cute. He was respectful, quiet, kind. All of us went out a few times with his church youth group."

It would have been around this time that bad things happened to Josh. He was raped, and his grandfather died, among other things. And, in turn, Komisarjevsky began to do bad things.

Julianne continued, "A few months later, my friend broke up with Josh. She found out that he was robbing houses, and couldn't abide that. That was the last I heard of him until last year, when I came into work on the twenty-third of July. My boss asked me excitedly, 'Did you hear what happened in Cheshire?' I hadn't, so we went onto the local news website, and there it was: triple murder on Sorghum Mill. Ten minutes from where I grew up. I asked my boss who did it, and she said, 'Someone from Cheshire.' We scrolled down the page, and I sucked in a huge breath of air. There it was, on the page: Josh Komisarjevsky. The boy with the unspellable last name. I was like, 'Oh, my God! I know him! I can't believe it.' He was such a nice kid."

Like the rest of Cheshire, Julianne spent most of that Monday online searching for updates on the tragedy. Eventually a news website posted Komisarjevsky's mugshot.

"There he was," she said. "Same eyes, same hair. He had a look on his face that said only one thing to me. He was sorry he got caught, but not sorry for what he did. I later heard from someone via [social networking website] Facebook who was friends with his girlfriend that he was stressing out. He had no money and had a court date the next week. He didn't know what he was going to do. I guess he finally thought of something."

Chapter 8:

Candlelight Vigil

On Monday, July 30, 2007, one week after the murders, a candlelight vigil was held outside Dr. Petit's medical practice on Whiting Street in Plainville. The doctor was there, sitting beneath a large white tent that had been erected in the middle of the street, between his mother and father, holding an unlit candle. The first to light his candle was Reverend John Brinsmade, pastor of Our Lady of Mercy Church in Plainville, which the elder Petits attend.

With great solemnity, Reverend Brinsmade lit Dr. Petit's candle.

The doctor then slowly stood, walked outside the tent and, one by one, used his candle to light the candles of the others. When he was done, about a hundred friends and neighbors held lit candles. Many hundreds more joined the gathering. They wept, prayed together, and sang "Amazing Grace."

Holding their candles, the group walked solemnly to a nearby park where a service was held. Dr. Petit's father-in-law, Reverend Richard Hawke, addressed the crowd: "With good, there is evil. Evil did not win July 23. When they beat Dr. Bill, they were beating God. God was there with those girls and their mother giving them strength and encouragement to get them through. Evil thought it had the upper hand, but look around at the goodness. Somewhere there's justice, and that evil will have to pay. Whether it be by man, it will certainly be, in the end, by God."

"It makes you want to give up on a world where this could happen to people like this, but then you realize they would not want us to give up," said family friend Deb Hereld. "If this happened to somebody else, the Petits would be the people in the front, comforting, organizing help, and just being there on a personal level. You don't meet many people like that in your life; you just don't. For the Petits, helping people was literally a way of life."

Plainville Town Manager Robert E. Lee addressed the crowd, saying, "Dr. William Petit and his family exemplify what is truly good about how we treat our fellow human beings and provide service to our communities. Over the years, the Petit family has touched the lives of many, many individuals in such a positive, caring way. This memorial service hopefully can begin the healing process for the Petit family and our community."

Other speakers included State Representative Elizabeth Boukus, Town Council Chairman Christopher Wazorko, several of Dr. Petit's Plainville High School class of 1974 classmates, and other family friends. During the speeches, Dr. Petit sat between his mother and father, William and Barbara. The doctor rose and embraced each speaker when he or she was finished.

Neighbor Kevin Mahan, who was at the vigil, said, "I think a lot of people are asking how God could let this happen."

Family friend James Richie said, "Plainville is unique and a wonderful place to live—largely because the Petit family has devoted itself to making it so."

Another family friend, Michael Majsak, said to Dr. Petit, "We are here for you. No request is too small. Let us know how we can give you strength to move through this tragic time."

William Petit Sr. said, "We've lost a good portion of our family; there's a tremendous hole. But there are other family members, including grandchildren, who remain. We need to go on for them."

Hereld recalled the day, eight years earlier, when Jennifer had learned she had MS. "Very unusual, she sounded choked up. And she explained that she had just been diagnosed with MS. But then it was like she kind of said, 'I'm just—I'm just having my little breakdown now, and then I'll just—I'll be okay.' And she was.

"Hayley was the respected girl. She was the girl who the kids would go to if they really wanted to know what was right to do. Hayley was an athlete, too. In crew, digging oars in for the final sprint was called 'giving it the Hayley ten.'"

Dr. Petit had mentioned Michaela's shy grin. Hereld knew just what he was talking about. "It was as though she had a really good secret." And she was always glued to the Food Network. "Rachael Ray was her favorite."

A friend of the Petits named Diane Brady told Robin Lee Michel of the *Plainville Citizen* of her last contact with Hayley.

"I made a scarf for Hayley and sent it to her so she would have it before she went away to school. Soon after, I received a handwritten thank-you note from Hayley saying she'd take it to college with her," Brady said. "That was the last communication I ever had from her."

People in central Connecticut and across the nation sought ways to express their grief and to offer their condolences. In many cases the way they chose was money. Donations to charities given to remember the Cheshire victims began to arrive within days of the murders, and were pouring in by the end of July.

Lisa Gerrol, president of the Greater Connecticut Chapter of the National Multiple Sclerosis Society, said that donations were coming in the mail and online, while pledges were arriving in an "overwhelming number of phone calls." On Tuesday, July 31, Gerrol said, "We have received $8,000 since Friday. People were so overwhelmed by the brutality of the incident that now it's just reassuring to Connecticut and to the community at large that the good in people is coming through now."

Gerrol talked about what an excellent fund-raiser Hayley had been for MS, and how she had been training Michaela to follow in her footsteps. "Hayley was teaching her younger sister about the ins and outs of fund-raising and organizing walk-a-thon teams. Michaela was already recruiting, excited to start her own walk team for the next MS Walkathon, May 2008.

Jamie Erickson explained why: "We can never fill their shoes, but it's an honor to work for something about which they were so passionate. They just touched our lives so much, and we wanted to give back a little bit of what they gave to us. We want to be here for Dr. Petit in any way we can—whether it's a hug or a smile. We believe we can raise a lot of money to help in the fight against multiple sclerosis because of the community and its love for the girls. Everyone wants to be a part of honoring their memory. Most are eager to fight for a cause—to make a difference."

Kathryn Thompson added, "We wanted to pick up on all the good that they left behind and keep carrying all of it."

Elizabeth Thompson explained, "We want to raise a lot of money. Dr. Petit and his family have been one of the best blessings in our lives. We are going to try to follow in Hayley and Michaela's footsteps and just be nice to everyone we come across in life. They were involved in the walk event to help find a cure—for their mom and others. They didn't do it for attention or accolades. They did everything with love. That's what inspires me most. Hayley and Michaela had big hearts."

Not all of the charitable donations have been toward MS. At the Cheshire Academy, several thousand dollars had been collected since the murders for a scholarship in Jennifer's name. School spokesman Philip Moore called the response "overwhelming." Requests for money for the fund were posted online and "a minute or two later" the money started to come in.

At Miss Porter's School, about fifty donors gave a total of $20,000 to a scholarship fund in Hayley's name. School spokeswoman Mara Braverman said, "It's a reflection of the depth of the tragedy and the sense of helplessness that we all feel that there is nothing we can do for these people except honor them and remember them. Very often in these situations we're looking for something to do. And doing something as positive as giving to a scholarship fund that will help some other young woman is a very positive action."

At the Chase Collegiate School in Waterbury, which both Hayley and Michaela had attended, a scholarship fund was being set up as well, but a spokeswoman at that school said that monetary figures were not available.

WNBC-TV in New York reported that Farmington Savings Bank was also accepting donations on behalf of the Petit Family Foundation. The foundation—set up by Dr. Petit's friends from the Plainville High School class of 1974—hadn't yet decided which causes to support, but Rick Healey, Dr. Petit's attorney and friend, said recipients would probably include MS, diabetes, and cancer organizations with which Dr. Petit was active.

Healey said, "There's a sense that there was such a large number of people out there who wanted to do something and to hopefully participate in something good coming from all of this tragedy."

With Dr. Petit's inspiring words and the candlelight vigil, the first light began to pierce the darkness of the tragedy, and from central Connecticut a glow of hope was growing.

Chapter 9:

More Search Warrants

On Tuesday, July 31, 2007, Judge Richard Damiani of the State of Connecticut Superior Court signed a search warrant allowing police to enter and search the Komisarjevsky home at 840 North Brooksvale Road in Cheshire for the following items:

> *Latex gloves, rubber gloves, cotton gloves, plastic zip ties, rope, restraining devices, dark-colored clothing, dark-colored caps and/or masks, items that may be related to the Petit residence and/or the Petit family, a laptop that may contain records of websites visited, downloads, data, plans, and files pertaining to the user committing the crimes of murder, kidnapping, and arson. Sketches, notes, and photographs pertaining to the Petit burglary. Any computers seized shall be submitted to the Connecticut State Police Computer Crime Unit for forensic examination and review. The forensic examination will include making true copies of the data and examining the contents of files.*

The affidavit requesting the search warrant was signed by Detectives James Canon and Joseph Vitello.

When the search warrant was executed by Detective Canon, he seized at the Komisarjevsky home twenty-one cable ties of various sizes, white in color. They were found in the kitchen drawer. The Komisarjevskys' laptop computer was taken, as were two brown cloth work gloves.

A second and third search warrants were drawn up, also by Canon and Vitello, seeking permission to search clothing items seized from Steven Hayes and Joshua Komisarjevsky and held at the Central District Major Crime Evidence Room in Meriden.

Since the evidence on the items and material being searched for was minute, sometimes microscopic, Hayes's clothes would be sent to the Connecticut State Police Forensic Laboratory for analysis. The lab had the equipment, personnel, and expertise to "conduct physical examination for scientific analysis, physical examination, biological and chemical testing, fingerprinting, photograph, criminalistic testing, and comparison, analysis, and reconstruction in order to locate, identify, compare, and reconstruct items of evidence and trace evidence to aid in establishing the circumstances of the crime and identity of the participants involved in the crime."

Because this search warrant dealt with the sexual aspects of the crimes against the Petits, it was released to the public only in redacted form.

A fourth warrant was drawn up requesting legal permission to seize "any and all account information associated with AT&T telephone number [deleted by author], including but not limited to all subscriber information, to include records, dates and times of any and all local [Automated Message Accounting or AMA tapes] and long-distance incoming and outgoing telephone numbers, billing record information, any additional telephone numbers associated with the account, any account identification information, and account history to include any and all master telephone numbers and billing records for the telephone number [deleted by author] for the period of July 22, 2007, at 0001 hours to July 24, 2007, at 0001 hours."

There was no guarantee that Komisarjevsky and Hayes were working alone in this criminal enterprise. For all law enforcement knew, the two they had caught might have been just the tip of a criminal iceberg. If the criminals were communicating with cohorts by phone during the attack, phone records would reveal that information.

The phone in question was the Petit house phone. It was known that at least one phone call was made from the Petit home during the home invasion. Police needed to know complete information about all incoming and outgoing calls from that phone during the key period of time.

The warrant would give the detectives permission to enter and search the local AT&T headquarters, specifically the office of the custodian of records, located at 310 Orange Street in New Haven.

Similar warrants were drawn up for the cell phone found in the road at the time of Komisarjevsky's apprehension and later determined to be his cell phone, and for the pink cell phone found in Komisarjevsky's pocket. The search warrant for the Petit house phone differed from the search warrant for the pink phone in the time frame for which records were being sought.

Information regarding the pink phone from July 16 through July 24 would be searched. The warrant for the pink phone requested permission for the police to search and seize information from CELLCO Partnership, DBA: Verizon Wireless. These offices were located at 20 Alexander Drive in Wallingford.

The wider time frame records for the pink phone were requested because, even though police suspected that the pink phone had been stolen from the Petit home, there was a chance that it had been taken during an earlier, undetected burglary, and therefore information during the days before the murders might be pertinent.

Also on July 31, Governor Rell announced that, from that point on, paroled burglars who had been convicted of breaking into occupied homes—there were thirty-eight of them in the state—would receive random visits from their parole officers.

She also said that she planned to ask the General Assembly to reclassify burglaries of occupied homes as violent crimes, which would mean that offenders would have to serve at least 85 percent of their sentences before parole became a possibility. Komisarjevsky had served less than 60 percent of his sentence and Hayes served 80 percent before they were paroled.

Chapter 10:

Angry Voices

As July turned to August, police continued to work the case. Even though, from a prosecutorial standpoint, the case might have seemed like a slam dunk, investigators needed to be thorough. When investigating a case this notorious, you don't want to miss anything.

Recent activity included the seizure of video surveillance tapes from the BP gas station where police believed the suspects had bought the gasoline they used as a fire accelerant, and from the Super Stop & Shop where the men had first crossed paths with Jennifer and Michaela.

When asked by a member of the press about the visit from investigators, a spokesman from the Super Stop & Shop confirmed that some evidence was taken but would not specify what the evidence was. A representative of the BP said cops were telling those to whom they talked not to give details to the press.

The BP spokesman did confirm, however, that if one of the suspects had purchased gas at the station sometime during the crime, he could have used the automated system, which meant the transaction could have been made without any contact with gas station employees. "If he used the automated system, there would be a credit or debit card record of the transaction," the spokesman said.

State Police Lieutenant Paul Vance also refused to speak in specifics. "We have seized any and all evidence that might be pertinent to establishing a timeline or any activities of these two [suspects] prior to the crime," Lieutenant Vance said. "We are collecting all of the information we can; that's all I can tell you."

Cheshire Police Department Lieutenant Jay Markella described the public's curiosity using this analogy: "Everyone's reading a book, but we've only read the first and last chapter, and they're trying to fill in the pages in between."

Vance said, "I also know that there have been questions about the response time by the Cheshire police to the first call for the case, and I can tell you there were no time issues at all. Eventually, when the case is complete, we'll be able to release more information, but not now. If anyone had any contact with these two, maybe they went into a store and bought a soda the day before, anything like that, we would like to know about it. We're trying to fill in every void we can."

On August 2, Governor Rell announced that she had directed the Board of Pardons and Paroles (BPP) to release all files in possession of the agency that are permitted to be released under law regarding the suspects in the Cheshire murders.

The governor directed Robert Farr, chairman of the BPP, to release the records immediately. In addition, she ordered that all parole hearings be publicly noticed and tape-recorded effective immediately. In the aftermath of the tragedy, initial reviews of policies and procedures of the BPP revealed that minutes were not recorded for every hearing.

"The only way to fix this process and to ensure in the future that the best and most appropriate decisions are made regarding paroles is to ensure that all information on offenders is available, not only to the board but also to members of the community," Governor Rell said. "The public has an absolute right to know the background of individuals being released into their cities and towns."

On July 31, Rell, Farr, and Department of Correction (DOC) Commissioner Theresa Lantz also announced a number of agreements to improve the process of information sharing between the judicial system and the BPP:

- Under the direction of Chief State's Attorney Kevin Kane, all police reports would now be provided to the BPP and the DOC at the time of sentencing.
- Under an agreement with the Court Support Services Division that had been in negotiation prior to the Cheshire tragedy, the BPP and the DOC would now be able to access all pre-sentence investigation reports electronically.
- All state's attorneys were to provide the BPP and the DOC with all sentencing transcripts, which would provide perspective from both the sentencing judges and victims.
- The BPP, the DOC, and the Court Support Services Division were negotiating an agreement that would provide the board with access to the juvenile records of all offenders.

"It is imperative that the officials making parole decisions have full and complete information on the offender, including statements of victims, prosecutors, defense attorneys, and the judge," Governor Rell said. "We can and must ensure that the full background on these individuals is taken into account during parole hearings."

As stories regarding police activities became public in greater detail, criticism increased of supposed mistakes made by Cheshire police following the 911 call from the Bank of America.

Critics pointed out that at least one officer was on the scene almost immediately, so fast that he might have come close to beating Steven Hayes and Jennifer as they returned from the bank. If that officer had raided the house immediately, the lives of the murder victims might have been saved. Instead, that officer waited outside the home for close to thirty minutes while police set up their perimeter and waited for members of the SRT team and equipment to arrive. It was estimated that twenty-five minutes elapsed between the time officers were told not to make contact with the Petit house and when the two assailants exited the house and tried to make an escape.

Why had police been so slow to approach the house?

Why did they need so many police to be present before they took action?

Why was a "special response" team needed?

Why did a "command center" need to be set up?

How many assailants did the Cheshire police believe were inside the Petit house?

No law enforcement officials would address these questions in public, although one did answer a reporter's questions under assurance of anonymity. The Associated Press quoted a local policeman as saying the reason for the hesitation was a statement made by the 911 caller that, according to Jennifer Hawke-Petit, the kidnappers were not going to harm anyone as long as police were not involved.

Lieutenant Jay Markella of the Cheshire Police Department granted an interview to a reporter from the *Hartford Courant*, during which he said, "The Cheshire Police Department's officers acted properly and according to their training. Based on the information that was received, the officers followed procedure and protocol."

ABC News contacted the head of the Toronto, Ontario, SWAT team to verify what a police force is supposed to do when there is a possible hostage situation. Barnie McNeilly, the Toronto police's top hostage negotiator, said the first thing the police should have done was to confirm that an actual hostage situation was under way, and that would mean making contact with the house. Only after the hostage situation had been verified should the police have set up a perimeter.

McNeilly said, "Of course, the appropriate response would depend on the precise information that the Cheshire police had at that time, which is not clear at the moment."

Since this was the real world and not a Hollywood movie, not everyone reacted to the murders in a manner that was supportive and sympathetic. In Hartford, Connecticut, a minister named Cornell Lewis complained about the extent of the furor over the Petit murders. He wondered why violent tragedies in urban centers such as Hartford did not stir up the same kind of media frenzy.

Speaking before a group of activists, Reverend Lewis said that he suspected that racism was at the root of it. The same thing was true with politicians, he argued. They did nothing about inner-city crime, but proposed new laws the instant a shocking crime took place in a small town or in the suburbs. Reverend Lewis said:

> *Governor Rell's response to urban violence has been slow as molasses, but she called for a review of the state's entire*

criminal justice system soon after the burglary and arson in Cheshire. Similar responses are needed when children die in Connecticut's inner cities. If we don't, then to me, it's sending a double message: one type of life, beautiful and white, is valued. Other kinds of life are not valued. There have been seventeen murders so far this year in Hartford. Last year, there were fifteen at this time in the year. Ten days before the Petit murders, two teens were shot to death execution-style in a botched robbery, yet those deaths garnered only a few newspaper articles and TV reports. Meanwhile, the Petit murders have become a national and international news story, with reporters struggling to hold back their own emotions. You see people with teary eyes, in the media, shaking hands and voices that seem to be wavering or quavering. When the two young boys were shot in the face, it was done professionally. It was hard-hitting and then that was it.

Although the minister had a point regarding government response, media experts said that he didn't understand what makes news *news*. In journalism school they teach students that a typical good news story is "man bites dog" because it is the opposite of what is expected. Gang killings in an inner city are absolutely tragic, but they are not big news because no one is shocked by them. A family being destroyed in a home invasion in Cheshire shocks everyone, and therefore makes the front page.

Francis Davila, a Latino community activist in Hartford, agreed with Reverend Lewis. He said, "The media coverage and government response to such tragedies should be equal. I think that it takes too long for something to happen when it comes to people of color. I'm not saying that nothing happens at all, but I think it takes too long. And I think when it happens in certain geographical areas, certain things happen quite quickly."

One media expert, Richard Hanley, assistant professor of journalism and director of graduate programs at Quinnipiac University's School of Communications, said that it was understandable why the Petit case had received such extensive coverage. The father was well known, the women were beautiful, a child was involved, and there was a sexual angle to the crime.

On the other hand, Hanley said, "I do think more work needs to be done in the cities in covering why a level of violence persists. And the media should look at how it covers these things. There's a sense that urban homicides are covered using 'drive-by journalism,' where reporters don't spend time learning more about the victims, the suspects, and the reasons behind the violence."

Chris Cooper, a spokesman for the governor, said, "Governor Rell cares about safety in all cities and towns. She has supported a variety of efforts to address gun crimes in the state's three biggest cities, along with enhanced state police presence, expanded job and educational opportunities for young people, and help combating gangs."

And then there were the opinions of the paranoid who saw a conspiracy under every rock. Most troubling among these were those who visited online chat rooms and tried to recruit believers for their "Dr. Petit was in on it" theory.

The logic here seemed to be that because his wife and daughters had been killed and he had not, then he must have had something to do with the crime, he must have hired those men—and the police and the government were helping him cover up his crimes.

Others condemned Dr. Petit for "abandoning" his family.

Still others blamed the Petits for not having a gun at home with which to defend themselves.

It was encouraging that, in chat rooms where such opinions were spouted, these rogue opinions were always, figuratively speaking, shouted down by the more clear-thinking crowd.

Chapter 11:

"I Came Here to See What Evil Looked Like"

It was ten in the morning on Tuesday August 7, 2007. The courtroom on the sixth floor of the State Superior Court in New Haven was packed. In the first two rows of the spectator section sat the close friends and family of William Petit.

This was to be the defendants' debut in the New Haven court, the court where they would, if all went according to plan, eventually face trial.

Dr. Petit himself was not in the courtroom. The supporters were maybe a dozen strong, and most of them couldn't mask their intense anger. The rest were grim.

To protect the two parolees from possible attack—"no Jack Rubys here" was the word—both men would be wearing bulletproof vests beneath their jumpsuits. They would be shackled at the wrists and ankles, making it difficult to walk. Police knew the courtroom would be thick with hostility. Komisarjevsky and Hayes might have been the most hated men in Connecticut history.

Everyone in the courtroom had to pass through tight security to get into the room—two checkpoints had been set up, and the public had to endure both. The first checkpoint was a metal detector. The second was a thorough search of briefcases and purses just outside the courtroom doors. In addition, men were frisked by a judicial marshal. A bomb-sniffing Labrador had scanned the courtroom for suspicious scents before any-one was allowed inside.

Outside the courthouse a state trooper with binoculars had kept watch while a half-dozen officers with rifles stood nearby, as TV cameras caught the accused being ushered into the build-ing through a back entrance.

The defendants were brought into the courtroom one at a time, Hayes first. Escorting the accused were Department of Correction special operations officers wearing camouflage clothing and black gloves.

As the shaved bald man was led in shackles into the court-room, a guard holding him by the arm, spectators fidgeted with nerves raw, jaws clenched, knuckles white, teeth grinding. Hayes, wearing an orange jumpsuit and chains, was only a few feet away. Hayes looked at the angry spectators as he entered, but he showed no emotion. Once he got to the front of the courtroom, he never looked back.

Some of the spectators moaned. Others gasped. Some tried to hold their tongues, but another lost control.

"Scumbag!" he said.

"Quiet!" Judge Richard A. Damiani said. "Whoever said that, take him out of here. Put him in the elevator and take him out of the building."

This was done. The heckler removed, a wall of uniformed marshals lined up between the defendant and the specta-tors. After a few moments all was quiet, and the proceedings commenced.

Hayes was represented by attorneys Patrick J. Culligan of Hartford and Tom Ullman of New Haven, both members of the state's chief public defender's office who specialized in capital cases.

Judge Damiani asked if Hayes waived his right to have the charges read aloud, and Hayes's counsel said they did. The judge then explained that Hayes had heard his rights read to him at his arraignment in Meriden.

"Do you understand your rights?" Judge Damiani asked Hayes.

Hayes said, simply, "Yes."

With that the judge ordered Hayes to be removed from the courtroom and that Komisarjevsky be brought in. As Hayes exited he kept his head up high, defiant. Whereas Hayes's guard had held his prisoner by the arm, Komisarjevsky's guard walked directly behind him.

Again, a spectator failed to hold his tongue.

"Killer!" shouted a young man. The judge again ordered that the man who had spoken be removed.

The proceedings for the second prisoner appeared ready to begin when it became apparent that not everyone was present. Komisarjevsky was to be represented by Jeremiah Donovan, a private lawyer appointed by the court. But Donovan was tardy, leaving Komisarjevsky standing alone.

The judge sensed the swelling enmity from the spectators as the suspect stood there alone without counsel, so he had Komisarjevsky taken out of the courtroom. Twenty minutes passed before Donovan arrived and apologized to the court. Komisarjevsky was then escorted back into the courtroom. This time there was no heckling.

Donovan asked the judge to recognize a second court-appointed attorney, Auden Grogins of Bridgeport, as his co-counsel on the case. The request was granted.

The judge again asked if the prisoner waived his right to have the charges read aloud. Donovan said he did. The judge then asked Komisarjevsky if he understood his rights, and Komisarjevsky said, "Yes."

And that was it. Neither man entered a plea. A probable-cause hearing was scheduled for September 18. Komisarjevsky was led back out of the courtroom. The younger of the defendants kept his head bowed.

The Petit family was allowed to leave through a private exit at the back of the courtroom.

The proceedings had not lasted long, but the tension in the courtroom had been so extreme that red flags were flying high in the minds of law enforcement. Trying these men was going to be a difficult process. Above and beyond the monumental task of impaneling an impartial jury, security was going to have to remain tight every time the defendants appeared in court. Hatred was so extreme that it was easy to imagine someone snapping and attacking the accused men.

After the brief court hearing, Lieutenant Vance of the Connecticut State Police said, "There were no threats. It was just a great deal of caution because of the high-profile nature of the case."

Melissa Farley, external affairs director for the state's judicial branch, added, "Due to the crowd and the nature of the crime, we had additional marshals in the courtroom. We wanted to make sure the proceedings moved smoothly."

A marshal who requested anonymity said, "There are crazies out there. We want to assure the accused men's safety and that of the public. With this kind of case and this kind of publicity, that's what's done."

In other words, no Jack Rubys.

Outside the courtroom many Petit supporters did not want to answer questions. A family representative did issue a statement for the press: "We understand that these men being arraigned have committed horrific acts of violence against our beloved family members, and that because those acts also violate numerous laws, the state has a responsibility to hold these individuals accountable for what they have done."

One supporter who was willing to speak was Nancy Manning, one of Dr. Petit's patients. She told a reporter from *ABC News*, "I came here to see what evil looked like."

Komisarjevsky's lawyer, Donovan, was practically smothered by a scrum of reporters. Although this would be his biggest case ever, Donovan was accustomed to representing defendants whose cases made the newspapers. He had earned a reputation as a tough lawyer in the mid-1990s when he defended members of a street gang on racketeering charges. In 2004 he defended a woman who was accused of vehicular homicide. The case involved a one-car crash on Route 9 in Cromwell. According to the prosecution, Donovan's client was driving the car and the man who had been a passenger was killed. The woman's defense was that she had not been driving the car at all. She claimed she had been the passenger, and that she had been administering oral sex to the driver at the time of the accident. She was acquitted by a jury.

Now, defending Komisarjevsky, Donovan was surrounded by reporters looking for a quote.

He said, "I have an uncontroversial, vanilla statement to make. It is a great responsibility to accept an appointment in a case like this. I myself live with a beloved wife and two lovely daughters. Nonetheless, I'll represent Joshua with all the vigor and ability I do possess. The court expects that of me. The prosecution certainly expects that of me, and the people of Connecticut expect that of me. If I do that, whatever the ultimate result is in this case, we can be confident that it will be a fair and just result."

Hayes's attorney, Patrick Culligan, who was the chief of trial services at the state's Public Defender Offices, did not make a statement, but when one reporter shouted to him, "How will your client plead?" Culligan barked back, "Not guilty!"

Up until this case, Culligan's most famous case was a defeat. He had represented accused killer Richard Lapointe, a mentally handicapped man who was charged with murdering his wife's grandmother. Lapointe denied murdering the woman yet signed a confession that had been written for him by police. Under Culligan's counsel Lapointe was convicted, but the case caused a sensation because of the question of whether or not he understood what he was signing when he "confessed."

The other side was talking, too. Prosecutor Michael Dearington made a brief statement for the gathered media: "I promise that the State will pursue this case to the fullest extent of the law allowable, making sure that the rights of the defendants as well as the rights of the victims and their family are not violated. I'd also like to say, on behalf of myself and my office, that our deepest thoughts and sympathies are with Dr. Petit and family members."

Following Hayes and Komisarjevsky's court hearing, there came fresh criticism of the system, which failed to protect the public from the two men who had turned out to be cold-blooded murderers.

Among the critics was seventy-three-year-old William A. Petit, Sr., the father-in-law and grandfather of the victims. A reporter contacted Petit at his home in Plainville, where he said, "No doubt about it, the system didn't work. It's too late now."

How long would it be before Hayes and Komisarjevsky actually faced trial for their alleged crimes? A representative from the state public defender's office said that they didn't expect jury selection to begin anytime before the summer of 2009, two years away. Since it was a capital case, both the state and the defense would cut no corners when preparing their cases. Nothing would be waived. Every step would be elaborate. No shortcuts. The defendants might be tried separately. Both sides would have many investigators working—and even once the trials got under way, they could take as long as a year to complete. To avoid appeals there would be excruciating attention to detail. If Hayes and Komisarjevsky made incriminating statements after their arrest, for example, were they properly informed of their Miranda rights beforehand? The case would cost millions of dollars and, because public defenders were being used, taxpayers would pay for both sides.

Even if, as expected, the men were convicted of triple murder, there would still be a lengthy sentencing hearing. "With death hanging over their heads, the State still has to build a case as to why they have to be put to death, and the defense a case as to why they should be spared," said Robert Nave, executive director of the Connecticut Network to Abolish the Death Penalty. "From their neonatal development to the time of the crime, it's all on the table."

It was suspected that, during Komisarjevsky's defense, the fact that he was adopted and sexually abused as a child would be emphasized for the jury.

Joe Lopez, an assistant public defender from New Haven, said the job of his office in this case was simple: to save the defendants' lives. "We have to do everything we can to make sure the defendants are not executed by lethal injection," Lopez said. "These are horrific crimes, but the State should not have the right to put them to death. We will pour all of our effort to block the death penalty."

Nave said, "The state could shorten the proceedings dramatically by arranging a plea bargain of life in prison without the possibility of release in exchange for guilty pleas. Otherwise, the trials and ensuing appeals would likely go on for twenty or more years."

That night on CNN, host Joe Pagliarulo asked Pat Brosnan, a former burglary detective who ran a security business, if there was anything in the profiles of Hayes and Komisarjevsky that would indicate an inclination to commit horrendous crimes such as the Petit murders.

Brosnan said that, because the pair had been convicted of committing so many crimes in the past, there was a chance that their known records were a mere fraction of their complete criminal résumé, and that the pair, either together or individually, had been violent in the past.

"Was this family stalked, do you think? Or did they just by chance go in here?" Pagliarulo asked.

Brosnan replied, "Well, it sounds like there was a stalking component, based on the timeline that was established, because they saw Michaela and Mrs. Petit at the store earlier in the afternoon. Evidently, they went to their residence, they followed them, they established where they resided. They then went shopping, purchased an air rifle and rope and returned and began the surveillance. When they thought that the time was right, which as it turned out was 3:00 A.M., they made their move. And that`s when it moved into a very serious home-invasion robbery. They batted down the father, and everyone knows what happened from there. It's worse than any B-movie horror film."

Brosnan called the situation "sheer madness," explaining that career burglars who strike when people are at home are "upping the stakes of the poker game," since inevitably a confrontation with residents will occur, and when it does, bad things usually happen.

Chapter 12:

Bartlem Park Rally and the Three-Strikes Controversy

Sadness in large part had shifted to anger. News that the suspects in the Petit murders were recent parolees steamed the residents of Cheshire, who held a rally on Wednesday, August 15, in Bartlem Park to keep repeat offenders in jail. About three hundred of the Petits' friends and neighbors attended. Dr. Petit and other family members were there as well.

One mother said, "We urge you to call your legislators, to sign a petition, to do something to keep us safe in our own homes at night while we sleep. I knew Jennifer Hawke-Petit because my son is a graduate of Cheshire Academy. He attended middle and upper schools there, and I think through all of those years he was a little bit in love with Jennifer. We all loved her. We all thought the world of her. We were all taking the cue from her, from her daughters, from her family to do what we can, in our own small way, to see that this kind of atrocity never happens again."

"How many innocent lives will be lost if we keep giving career criminals chance after chance after chance?" asked another mother. "Lawmakers, we urge you tonight, close the revolving prison doors permanently for those criminals with long and violent records. Burglars, strangers who come into our homes, who come into our safe havens—this is the definition of violent and indecent. We are left here feeling defenseless and violated, and most of us are left living in fear. Even though this terrible tragedy occurred in the town of Cheshire, remember, it could have happened in any one of our towns. I'd like to end with a quote, something that Dr. Petit wrote in his Notice of Appreciation. He has asked us to 'go forward with the inclination to live with the faith that embodies action,' to love your family, to help a neighbor, and to fight for a cause."

Jessica Ryan was one of the neighbors who circulated a petition online calling for stricter laws. She told a reporter from the *New York Times*, "I don't think it is asking too much to protect those you love by helping this to never happen again."

The online petition drew 42,646 signatures. The petition called for "mandatory life sentences" for those convicted of three felonies.

Ryan edited a local paper called the *Cheshire Herald*. In an editorial she wrote for that paper, she asked, "Why is it that our government continues to push this issue aside and refuses to admit that we need to take action?"

Marilyn Bartoli, one of the rally's organizers, told a reporter, "I'm not telling lawmakers how to do their job, but what we have is not working. Both of the men arrested in this case have long records for burglary and a history of recidivism, yet records show they were not treated as serious offenders by the criminal justice system." Bartoli had a child who attended Cheshire Academy, and like so many others, she noted that Jennifer Hawke-Petit was more than just the school nurse, but a proxy mom as well. "I think people actually tried to be sick in order to be around her. She was that kind of woman," she said.

Both Komisarjevsky and Hayes had been deemed to be appropriate candidates for supervised parole in the community, based on their criminal history that involved a minimum level of violence. Both men reported weekly to parole officers and fully complied with the requirements of their release.

Speakers at the rally said that they wanted the laws in Connecticut to be changed, strengthened, so that they were more like California's repeat-offender laws. The California statute is informally referred to as the Three-Strikes-You're-Out Law.

It is considered one of the strictest in the nation. That law calls for an automatic twenty-five-year-to-life sentence for the third felony conviction of an offender whose previous convictions were for violent or serious felonies. Under Connecticut's current "persistent serious felony offender law," enacted in 1994, a prosecutor can seek a longer sentence if the offender has been convicted and incarcerated for one previous felony.

A call for stricter laws after a particularly horrible crime has been committed is human nature, but Connecticut State Representative Michael P. Lawlor, a Democrat from East Haven who was the state's co-chairman of the legislature's Judiciary Committee, said, "Even California's law would not have kept these two suspects in jail. Komisarjevsky had just one previous felony conviction despite his arrests in a rash of residential nighttime burglaries. In Mr. Hayes's case, a prosecutor had not taken the opportunity to seek a longer sentence for a subsequent conviction. But even if Hayes had committed his crimes in California, they would not have triggered the automatic twenty-five-years-to-life sentence because they are not considered violent or serious felonies in that state." The legislature's Judiciary Committee will begin looking at three-strike models from other states, including California, on September 11. The committee will receive a briefing from state criminal justice officials about its current sentencing and re-entry process. The committee will also gather information about the costs of programs in other states and will hear about possible sites for new prison facilities."

Only twenty-eight criminals were in jail under Connecticut's persistent offender law at the time of the Cheshire murders. The state's total prison population at the time was in excess of 19,000, according to the Connecticut Department of Correction.

The circumstances of those twenty-eight prisoners varied greatly. They had been convicted of crimes ranging from probation violations to murder, and their sentences ranged from six months to eighty years. Only one of the twenty-eight was considered a "dangerous persistent felony offender" and he had been sentenced to thirteen years in 2002 for third-degree burglary.

Bruce Carlson, a board member of Survivors of Homicide, a Connecticut-based organization of families who have lost a loved one to murder, said, "The courts have very wide discretionary powers over when to apply the enhanced stiff sentences to repeat offenders. The current process is much too loose."

James Papillo, a Connecticut victim's advocate, announced that he had proposed the Petit Home Invasion Act, which would reclassify home invasion as a serious felony offense. "My proposal was designed to be very tough on repeat offenders," Papillo said. "The reclassification, in addition to a tougher persistent-offender law, would begin to solve some of the problems."

There were Connecticut citizens who feared "Big Brother" watching. Others wanted Big Brother to watch more closely, and there were calls for, in light of the Petit murders, future parolees being forced to wear GPS devices so that their location could be tracked via satellite twenty-four hours a day.

Putting civil liberty issues aside for a moment, how practical was the idea?

Would the GPS systems be put in place for all parolees, for the rest of their lives? For, if the systems were temporary, wouldn't the parolees simply wait until they had been removed—as Komisarjevsky had waited for his electronic surveillance device to be removed—before resuming their criminal careers?

And, how many man-hours would be needed to track the location of all of the state parolees?

And how, being observed from outer space, would normal day-to-day behavior distinguish itself from criminal behavior?

By the end of August, the Petits' neighbors had just about had it with reporters knocking on doors and asking questions. When Marianne O'Donnell from the cable news station MSNBC drove around Sorghum Mill Drive looking for people willing to comment, she was greeted with out-and-out hostility.

Fifteen doors slammed in her face without comment.

The sixteenth said, "We're sick of you media coming around here knocking on our doors. We're trying to heal. But how can we when you guys keep coming, asking these questions?"

Few benefit from tragedies such as that which befell the Petit family. But among those who did benefit were those who sold guns and security systems. And, for the most part, nobody begrudged these industries the profits they made.

But one national alarm company crossed the line when it used the Petit murders in its advertising. The offending company was ADT Security Services, Inc. This was the company that, in the days following the murders, distributed leaflets in the Petits' neighborhood with the headline: "A Sign of the Times."

According to company spokeswoman Ann Lindstrom, "Prompted by the tragic attack on the Petit family, the ADT Wallingford office received numerous requests for information from people interested in electronic security systems to help protect themselves and their families from a similar violent attack. ADT was responsive to the inquiries received from the community by providing them with information and risk assessments. Members of the community expressed gratitude to ADT for our prompt response, while others were critical of us."

Connecticut officials didn't hear much of the gratitude, but they heard plenty of the criticism.

Jerry Farrell Jr., the commissioner of Connecticut Consumer Protection, said, "Many homeowners were offended and believed the timing and contents of the flyers were in poor taste. When I heard about ADT leafleting the neighborhood and saw the flyer in question I was outraged. While one cannot say that the flyer was false, the timing and nature of it was totally inappropriate."

In the face of the criticism, the company made a public statement that it "never meant to offend." To atone for its indiscretion, on August 18, 2007, the company agreed to donate $1,000 to the National Multiple Sclerosis Society.

Chapter 13:

A New Cohesion in Deaconwood

While much of central Connecticut was dealing with its pain by raising money for the causes cherished most by the Petit women, the Deaconwood section of Cheshire, those who lived closest to the crime, were dealing by huddling closer together. They were talking a lot less to reporters but a lot more to one another.

The neighborhood had not been as close as it could have been before the tragedy. Not everyone knew everyone else's name. But all of that had changed. Now, under the initiative of the Averack family, there was an e-mail list, a neighborhood directory. Everyone knew everyone else's name—not to mention their e-mail and snail-mail addresses. At the vigils and memorials and rallies that were held, Deaconwood residents now requested that they all sit together.

As Pam Averack put it, "We've been through a lot. This shakes you out of the idea that we are independent. We are not strangers anymore."

Pam's husband Robert said, "Now we see one another on a more personal level. One of the important lessons we learned was that it's really good to be in a community. It's really good to have people you know who can be there if you need them.

"Our lives have become so much more complex and consumed by trying to make a living, by keeping up with family and friends, by keeping up with massive amounts of information that we are bombarded with. We hadn't really taken the time to know about one another as a family. That's created a really depersonalized society. When you put it all together, it tends to create greater anonymity between neighbors, and that's sad because that's not the way it was when we were growing up.

"I don't think anyone had in mind that life should become so consumed with getting through the day and shuttling our children to the soccer fields that we lose touch with the very fabric of what makes life worth living."

Neighbor Tamara Epstein, who lived four houses away from the Petits, said, "I can't tell you how many more neighbors I've met. We wave to each other more. We're looking out for each other more."

Tamara was the creator of the three-bead "Unity" pin to designate Deaconwood residents. She made a bunch of the pins and put them in a bag attached to her mailbox. Now when neighbors who all but ignored one another before meet in the grocery store, they stop and chat.

One of the reasons Deaconwood had grown socially distant was that many of the original residents, who had been there for thirty years, had not bothered to befriend the families who had moved in more recently. But all of that started to change at the first candlelight vigil.

Original Deaconwood resident Maddy Tannenbaum recalled:

> *I knew all the people on my block, but there was no reason for me to interact with the new people. At the candlelight vigil I met people I never knew before—wonderful people. Now when I walk by, I'll stop and say hello. I make it a point to wave.*
>
> *Before, I didn't feel attached to the Deaconwood community. Now we're defined by our neighborhood again. People*

are committed to having a stronger neighborhood. People moved here for these kinds of relationships.

I moved to this neighborhood because it was a neighborhood. I walk these streets. These are my streets. This is my neighborhood. I want the cohesiveness back again.

I want all the kids to use my mailbox as home plate. If it means they have to run in my driveway to kick that ball, hey, run in my driveway. This has rekindled the feeling that we need a neighborhood and we are a neighborhood.

In Deaconwood many tiny sparks had now joined to form one bright light.

Chapter 14:

The Congregation's Dilemma

The Petit murders put the congregation of Cheshire's United Methodist Church in a difficult political position. The Petits' church had been politically active for years and had taken positions on a number of controversial topics of the day, such as the state of refugees living in Meriden and poverty in El Salvador.

One of those positions was that they were on record as being against the death penalty. The church's last three pastors were all vocally opposed to capital punishment. The church held classes that taught "restorative justice."

Yes to rehabilitation, no to punishment. That was their motto. When the State of Connecticut executed a prisoner for the first time in forty-five years in 2005, the church held a midnight vigil outside the prison.

Then came the Petit murders. Not sure what to say, many United Methodist parishioners kept their mouths shut. Just about everyone was reexamining their views on capital punishment. Should they remain quiet? Should they protest whatever punishment was given to the men who killed the Petits? Should they find out how Dr. Petit felt about the matter and then follow his lead?

Reverend Stephen E. Volpe, the church's pastor, was as anti-capital punishment as they come. "I'm treading lightly out of respect for the Petit family," Reverend Volpe said. "I do not feel we, in this church, ought to make this tragedy the rallying cry for anything at this point."

Before the murders, the church had scheduled an anti-capital punishment speaker, but canceled that engagement out of sensitivity to the Petit family. The church usually collected money during the holidays to send presents to prison inmates. There was talk of canceling that offertory for 2007.

It was commonly believed by those who had worshipped beside her that Jennifer Hawke-Petit was against the death penalty and that she would not have wanted her killers to be executed.

Carolyn Hardin Engelhardt, who in addition to being part of the United Methodist congregation was director of the ministry resource center at Yale Divinity School Library, offered her opinion: "It'd be so dishonoring to her life to do anything violent in her name. That's not the kind of person she was."

Although it wasn't confirmed, some members of the church believed that Jennifer may have signed a document called the Declaration of Life, which requests, in the case of one's own murder, that the prosecution not seek the death penalty. According to the *New York Times,* thousands of people have signed the document, including former governor of New York Mario Cuomo and actor Martin Sheen.

Lucy Earley said that she saw a few churchgoers sign the document, and she believed Jennifer was among them. "She was a nurse and she would not cause harm to anyone," Earley said.

If such a document were to surface, experts said, it might serve as a rallying point for those opposing capital punishment but would have little or no effect on the prosecution of Hayes and Komisarjevsky.

According to Waterbury veteran prosecutor John A. Connelly, who was not involved in the Petit case, "Our job is to enforce the law no matter who the victim is or what the victim's religious beliefs are. If you started imposing the death penalty based on what the victim's family felt, it would truly become arbitrary and capricious."

Michael Dearington, who was involved in the prosecution in this case, has refused to comment on the subject of the Declaration of Life document.

Nobody knew how Dr. Petit felt about capital punishment. He had spoken at gatherings in support of his family and at the public service held in their honor, but he had not answered any questions. Some knew that Dr. Petit attended the Methodist church because Jennifer, being a reverend's daughter, was a Methodist. Bill himself was Roman Catholic.

Still, "he was a member in everything but name only," said the Reverend George C. Engelhardt, who was the congregation's pastor for twenty-nine years before becoming superintendent for several churches in the region. The reason many didn't know that Bill was Catholic was that he couldn't have been more active in United Methodist events. When the church had a living nativity in its parking lot the previous Christmas, all four Petits had participated. Even with his family gone, Bill continued to attend United Methodist services. His daughters' friends always sat with him and took turns placing a hand of support on his shoulder.

Of course, Bill's entire family had been active in the church. Jennifer taught Sunday school, while Michaela played the flute and sang during services. Hayley proved to be excellent with a set of tools when the church's Teen Brigade went around town doing home improvements for disabled persons.

Dr. Phil Brewer, a member of the congregation who had spoken to Dr. Petit since the murders, believed that Dr. Petit was "strongly in favor of executing these guys. He has nothing against members of the congregation who are against the death penalty, but he would not take it kindly if our congregation as a whole took a position against the death penalty. It would be seen as an effort to force him into choosing between being part of the congregation or wanting to have the death penalty."

Dr. Brewer remembered that, during a memorial service held in September, Dr. Petit had read the prayer of Saint Francis of Assisi, and seemed to pause at the phrase, "Where there is injury, pardon."

"What really took my breath away when he cited the Prayer of St. Francis and either lingered on the word 'pardon' or got stuck on the word 'pardon,'" Dr. Brewer said. "There was a long pause after he spoke the word, and to me, that signaled that this was on his mind."

Dr. Brewer's wife, Dr. Karen Brown, interjected, ""I think it's what he wants to feel, but it's hard to get there."

Reverend Diana Jani Druck, who ran the church from 2001 to 2005, said the Petit murders were a strong test for the congregation because the case lacked many of the factors that people most frequently used to argue against the death penalty. Since the criminals and the victims were all white, the argument that blacks were more likely to be put to death than whites did not apply. Because the men were captured fleeing the murder scene, it was unlikely that there was a case of mistaken identity or that the wrong men had been arrested.

Plus, Reverend Druck added, the congregation was angry over the murders, and it was human nature to want vengeance under such circumstances.

Many knew that sooner or later the church was once again going to have to face the subject of capital punishment. But the time had not yet arrived. The wounds to the community were still too fresh.

Another member of the United Methodist Church who was struggling with his long-held beliefs about capital punishment was Richard Hawke, Jennifer's seventy-six-year-old father, who had retired with his wife to Florida but still spent his summers in Pennsylvania.

He confided to a reporter that both he and Jen's mom, Marybelle, had been searching the Bible for answers and doing a lot of praying. He'd told a prosecutor in the case of his daughter and granddaughters' murders that the killers "had no right to continue to live in society."

After searching church doctrine, he came to the conclusion that, although for the most part his church was against capital punishment, it did leave room for "individual conscience" in cases involving "children and rape."

Hawke told a reporter, "I don't think people can imagine the terror that went through the lives of these three women during the hours they were held hostage. Our kids weren't just shot. They were tortured and terrorized. I couldn't get past that. Those women represented everything that was the opposite of those that took their lives. They were the epitome of good, and the others were the epitome of evil."

Marybelle worried that, because of the leniency of Connecticut law, the killers may one day walk the streets again. "I think the crimes they committed have merited the loss of their lives or lifetime punishment," she said. "I would always prefer for there to be lifetime punishment, but I don't have enough faith in the justice system that they would be held to lifetime in prison."

The Hawkes were asked if their daughter had signed a Declaration of Life document, as had been rumored. Neither knew for sure. "No one can positively say they saw her sign that and give it back to anyone," her father said, "She may have taken it home. It's probably burned up in the fire."

Richard and Marybelle both said that they were grateful for the number of years they had with their lost loved ones. They expressed fond memories of when Hayley and Michaela would visit them in Florida and together they would go to a wild animal park.

Richard concluded, "We will be in a type of prison for the rest of our lives because of the loss of our loved ones."

On Monday, September 17, 2007, a court hearing was held in New Haven regarding the Petit murders, but, because of security issues experienced in the past, both Hayes and Komisarjevsky waived their right to attend the hearing.

The judge and lawyers quickly ran through the routine business. A hearing scheduled for the following day to determine probable cause was postponed. Judge Damiani announced that he would make a ruling on the release of sealed documents on October 16. Among the documents under seal were eleven search warrants that contained comments that defense attorneys thought were "extremely prejudicial" and might hinder the possibility of getting their clients a fair trial.

The release of the documents had been requested by *The Hartford Courant*. The prosecution said it had no objection to the release of the documents, as its investigation was complete.

The sleepless nights were growing cooler and the days shorter. And so the summer ended with the pain unabated and the fear undiminished.

Chapter 15:

Autumn

On Wednesday evening, September 19, 2007, at 7:00 p.m., Cheshire residents once again got together to show their support for Dr. Petit and to honor his lost family. A memorial service was held by the town of Cheshire at the Cheshire High School football field, and the bleachers were filled with supporters.

Cheshire Town Manager Michael Milone addressed the gathering:

> *Good evening. We are gathered together to honor the lives and the memory of Jennifer, Hayley, and Michaela Petit, to send our condolences and to extend our sympathy to Dr. Petit and the Petit and Hawke families, and to help this community through the healing process.*
>
> *Jennifer, Hayley, and Michaela's goodness and generous spirit have had a most profound effect on all of us. Their legacy will be their strong, positive, and life-affirming qualities that will be memorialized in our hearts and through the fund established in their honor.*
>
> *To the Petit and Hawke family, we as a community cannot possibly express the immense sadness and sympathy and heartache that we feel. We grieve for you. We are here to display our feelings and our support.*

"We hope that in some small way," he concluded, addressing Dr. Petit now, "this helps you and your family.

Dr. Sandra Wirth, the interim head of school at Cheshire Academy, said, "Earlier this month, our school celebrated the lives of the Petit women at a memorial service for our students, many of whom were away during the events of the summer. Tonight, we are very grateful to be part of this town memorial, which shows the influence of the Petit family throughout Cheshire, throughout Connecticut, and, as we have learned through the many international messages of sorrow and support that we have received, throughout the world. All three were our friends and members of our family. And we recognize that their influence went well beyond the hedges of the Cheshire Academy."

Reverend Volpe said, "What made Jennifer, Hayley, and Michaela so unique was their love, their love of people, their love of life, and their love of doing whatever they could for others. We have all become better people for having known them."

Dr. Petit then spoke. As he had in the past, he again proved himself unafraid to share his innermost thoughts. In a tired but clear voice, he said, "I still struggle every day after fifty-eight days, and I'm not sure that will ever change. On that day in July, all that was good in my life was taken from me by total evil, Satan on Earth. I still turn to Jennifer to ask if she remembers a date, but she's not there. I turn to ask Hayley how her French class went and how crew practice was, and she's not there. I turn to hug KayKay Rosebud and ask if they finally served something she liked for lunch and if the boys behaved in gym class that day, but she's not there.

"I struggle to find meaning. I always encouraged my children to support causes, to do volunteer work and help others. I hope it is in the girls' lives and how they lived each day and what they lived for. They found much meaning in their lives by helping others. I hope Cheshire will be known for its good people and its good works."

After the ceremony, neighbor Chris Rao remembered how alive the Petit household had been:

The first to knock on the door and greet us when we were new neighbors were baby Hayley and Bill. Bill held a full-sized basketball, an appropriate gift for my two-and-a-half-year-old son.

I remember years later how Hayley and Michaela had a Laura Ashley lemonade stand decorated with a tablecloth and served ice-cold lemonade and fresh-baked brownies and cookies. They put two boys down the street who had a less professional lemonade stand right out of business.

I knew Jen even before we became neighbors. I'd worked for her as a nurse at Yale–New Haven Hospital. She inspired the younger nurses. She was always stylish. She favored black and white and fine fabrics. She made sun-bleached salmon look great.

I remember the Petit home as cozy and unpretentious, with a peachy salmon wallpaper in the living room, Christmas lights, and Bill always planting outside or filling the bird feeders. When I think of them I have pain in my chest and tears in my eyes—but also a smile in my heart.

On Monday, October 23, 2007, copies of the search warrants granted in the days following the murders were made public for the first time, and those who were curious learned a few new details about the crime that had not been previously available.

For example, one warrant included the information that Jude Komisarjevsky had been suspicious that her son was up to no good when he left home late at night wearing a hooded sweatshirt and claiming that he had to "see an individual about a job."

The public learned that within an hour of the arrests, police found a 1998 Chevrolet van owned by Jude Komisarjevsky parked in the parking lot of a condo complex called Quarry Village. Inside the van was the BB gun purchased at Wal-Mart, rubber gloves in various colors, and a dark shirt with eyeholes cut into it so it could be used as a mask. A search of the Petits' 2005 Chrysler Pacifica revealed that it too contained latex gloves. Also found in the SUV were cotton gloves and four sets of interlocking plastic zip ties such as those that had been used to bind Dr. Petit's wrists and ankles during the crime.

Another search warrant requested permission to search Hayes's pickup truck, which had been left in the Stop & Shop parking lot. In the truck were found Hayley's backpack and wallets belonging to Bill and Jennifer.

The First Annual Petit Family Foundation Golf Tournament was held on Monday, October 15, 2007, at the Country Club of Farmington in Farmington, Connecticut. The tournament was a shotgun start. That meant that everyone was assigned to start at a different hole and, when a shotgun was fired, everyone started at the same time. The advantage to this was that everyone finished more or less at the same time and didn't miss any post-tourney festivities (dinner, awards, and a raffle). The start was 11:00 a.m.

Donations ranged from $2,500, which earned the sponsor four greens fees, dinner with reserved seating, two tee-box sponsor signs, and special program recognition, down to $75, which earned the sponsor dinner only. The organizer for the event was Steve Zarmsky, who worked at the Farmington Savings Bank.

Up until the end of October 2007, just about everyone assumed that the men who murdered the Petits planned to spend the money Jennifer withdrew from the bank to support their drug habits. But there was one person who had a different theory. She was eighteen-year-old Caroline Mesel, who had graduated from Ellington High School in 2007. Ellington was a suburb of Hartford. Caroline's father was a minister and had been the pastor at Ellington Wesleyan Church.

Caroline said that she had inside information because she had been Joshua Komisarjevsky's girlfriend, and maybe the $15,000 was actually meant to get her back.

Joshua and Caroline had been together between Joshua's last release from prison and shortly before the Petit murders, when the Mesel family moved to Rogers, Arkansas—a large town in the extreme northwest corner of the state, near both the Oklahoma and Missouri borders—where, after fifteen years in Ellington, her father had accepted an invitation to pastor the Rogers Wesleyan Church.

According to Caroline, Joshua had been very upset that she was moving away, and she remembered him sitting on his bed writing down numbers, trying to figure out how much money each of them would have to make in order to "bring her back" to Connecticut.

The figure he came up with was $15,000.

Caroline claimed Joshua had said to her, "I'd rob a bank to get you back." She thought at the time that he was joking. She'd told him not to be funny. Now she wasn't so sure he was kidding at all.

"At first I thought it was to get me back, but he probably just did it for the hell of it. It could have been for anything," she said. "He phoned me from prison a week after the murders and we talked for about a half hour. He blamed Hayes. He said Hayes was out of control and said they had to kill the women because they were witnesses. He was just telling me that Hayes freaked out. He kind of tried to make Hayes look like he did it all. He told me how he and Hayes attacked the man [Dr. Petit]. He said he was a big man and they didn't think they could take him, so they hit him with a baseball bat. It was kind of like he was bragging."

He told her that, during the early morning hours of the attack, Jennifer had offered to make breakfast for him and Hayes as they waited for the bank to open.

Caroline said she asked him if he raped any of the victims and he said no.

"He said he was sorry and he still loved me," Caroline said.

The girl explained that she had met Komisarjevsky during his last stint in prison. She had gone to the prison with her big sister to visit him. Her sister, she said, had previously dated him. The older sister met him years before at a Christian camp in Maine.

Reverend Norm Mesel, Caroline's father, explained how Caroline and Joshua met.

"Caroline's older sister Clairees met Josh at a Christian camp where I was the keynote speaker in September of 1993," he said. "They remained friends throughout the years. In fact, it was Clairees who unintentionally introduced Caroline to Josh. Clairees wanted to see Josh while he was in prison to encourage him, and she took Caroline along with her for company. Unbeknown to any of us, Caroline and Josh began a pen-pal relationship."

Reverend Mesel said that Komisarjevsky had explained to Caroline that he would need $15,000 to bring her back to Connecticut.

"In one of his final phone calls to her before the crime, he talked about a business deal to raise the money," Reverend Mesel said. Regarding the amount of $15,000, he said, "There's something about that dollar amount. He did make the comment that whatever he did he did for her."

But why $15,000? How would that bring her back?

"That is the $15,000 question that just might help us better understand what led to this horrible crime," said Reverend Mesel. "Josh told Caroline months before she left for Arkansas that she needed to raise $15,000 before she could return to Connecticut. Many times my wife and I heard that $15,000 was needed. We both asked, 'What for?' but never received a satisfactory answer. I even told Caroline on several occasions that she wasn't going to raise $15,000 for anyone. Such a demand was ridiculous.

"Of course, I interpreted this as Josh's way of saying, 'Out of sight, out of mind,' knowing perfectly well that raising $15,000 was an impossibility.

"On Saturday night, around 11:00 p.m., just four hours prior to entering the Petit home, Caroline was able to reach Josh by cell phone and discovered he was in either a bar or restaurant with another individual, and Josh told her that he was working out a business deal worth $15,000 so that she could come back to Connecticut. She just figured that he was with another woman and he was trying to get her off the phone.

"When we received news of the crime and heard that Mrs. Petit was forced to withdraw $15,000, all kinds of flags went up. There is something about that exact dollar amount, but nobody knows what."

Caroline said that when she spoke to Komisarjevsky just hours before the Petit home invasion, she sensed that something was terribly wrong. "He seemed kind of jumpy and wanted to get somewhere and do something," she said.

The next morning, she said, Komisarjevsky's mother called her and said that she was worried. "She told me he'd gone out in dark clothing. I kept calling him that day but I couldn't get through. I just had this gut feeling that something was wrong," she said.

Now that she knows the kind of actions Komisarjevsky is capable of, she can't believe she ever liked him. Memories of him now haunt her. During their relationship he gave her clothes and pictures. She has thrown them all out. "The only presents from him I kept was the jewelry, and I plan on selling that," she said. "I think he's just a low-down punk and he deserves whatever he gets. If they had a poll I'd actually push for the death penalty."

Caroline's dad had his opinions of Josh, too. "I have met Josh on numerous occasions—our family has had a fifteen-year history with Josh spanning his friendship with both Clairees and Caroline," said Reverend Mesel. "Josh even helped pack our U-Haul before we left for Arkansas.

"I always treated Josh with respect but never trusted him or had any appreciation for him. Most of my apprehension with Josh centered around broken promises he made to Clairees over the years, and I was the one trying to mend her broken heart.

"Also, I had my reservations regarding Josh because I felt that he was going to be a career criminal. Never did I imagine he would be violent, but I felt with his drug habit that he would constantly be breaking and entering or stealing in some fashion.

"I told Josh when I discovered that he was dating Caroline exactly how I felt about him and that I even thought he was a *pedophile*. Caroline may now be eighteen—soon to be nineteen—but *she looks like she is fourteen*. Josh never changed his mood when I shared these observations—which really did concern me. He seemed to be a life without a soul.

"My entire family's lives have been extremely altered because of our association with Josh. From constant calls by the media, interviews with law enforcement agents, and the overwhelming ache and pain every time we see or hear the details of what the Petit family endured. We will never again be the same. There are those who feel that God moved us to Arkansas at precisely the right time because maybe our daughter also could have been a tragic statistic in all of this. But again, even though I had little to no appreciation of Josh, I never would have imagined him involved in a crime so horrific as this."

On October 30, 2007, Komisarjevsky appeared in New Haven Superior Court before Judge Damiani. He waived his right to a probable cause hearing and, when asked how he pleaded to charges of murder, kidnapping, sexual assault, and arson, he said, "Not guilty."

Two days later, Hayes appeared in court, looking noticeably thinner, and also officially denied his guilt. Each hearing only took about ten minutes, and, as had been the case every time the defendants were brought into court, security was stringent.

Hayes's lawyers accused the Cheshire Police Department of leaking details of the case to a local newspaper. Lieutenant Jay Markella of the Cheshire police said the allegations were unsubstantiated.

On Tuesday, November 6, 2007, citing inflammatory and prejudicial articles that had been running in the local newspapers, Judge Damiani imposed a gag order, forbidding defense and prosecuting attorneys "and all agents working for them" from speaking with the press.

The order was requested by Hayes's attorney, Patrick Culligan. He said that twenty-three instances in one *Hartford Courant* story, plus even more in an Associated Press dispatch that had come out at the same time, were evidence of "leaks that are prejudicial to the court's ability to find an impartial jury."

Representing *The Hartford Courant* in the matter was attorney David Atkins, who had been trying to get documents in the case unsealed. Atkins immediately objected to the gag order, saying the judge couldn't rule on information already printed.

"The court must look at the future to determine if there is any information that might be printed in the days to come that would do any damage," Atkins said.

Judge Damiani said that he felt the gag order was necessary to preserve the jury pool. He said that he had considered alternatives, such as a lengthy *voir dire* (jury selection) process to weed out potential jurors who were familiar with the case because of press reports.

The judge added, "But I myself have had people approach me and ask how the defendants could possibly plead not guilty, which tells me that a *voir dire* process may not be a reasonable alternative, but we will cross that bridge when we get to it. A change of venue for the case is not an option because the case has been covered nationally."

Atkins complained that Judge Damiani's ruling was an affront to the First Amendment.

"Any time the government restricts the media's news-gathering ability, it's a step backward for free speech," Atkins said. "It is unclear how long the judge intends the gag order to last. And I don't know if it applies to police departments other than the state police and the Cheshire Police Department."

In Plainville there was a florist called The Pink Door and Company Flowers and Gift Shop. The shop was at 36 Whiting Street, on the same street as Dr. Petit's medical office, and the same street on which William Petit Sr. had long owned a small store. In mid-November the florist came up with an idea to raise money for the Petit Family Foundation. In honor of what would have been Michaela's twelfth birthday on November 17, the shop sold bouquets of roses and rose bushes in her honor, with the money going to charity. Rose was Michaela's middle name, and now each rose sold became a light, pink and white and red, battling the darkness of despair.

Chapter 16:

Dr. Petit Writes a Letter

On November 26, 2007, Dr. Petit wrote a letter to the leaders of the Connecticut State Judiciary Committee. The letter was addressed to Senator Andrew J. McDonald, Chair; Representative Michael Lawlor, Chair; Senator John A. Kissel, Ranking Member; and Representative Arthur J. O'Neill, Ranking Member.

It read:

My life changed profoundly 126 days ago. From the thousands of communications I have received from so many people in and outside Connecticut, I understand that others' lives have also been changed. Those horrible events not only took the lives of my beautiful and wonderful wife and daughters, but they also exposed some glaring defects in our laws and their inability to adequately ensure our public safety. Every resident of Connecticut deserves to have those glaring deficiencies in our public safety laws corrected fully and promptly.

It is my understanding that you are meeting to review those deficiencies, and to address how best to deal with them. I know that the legislative process and the political process are closely intertwined. I firmly believe that political considerations should have no place in this debate. From my perspective, the sole issue and the only legitimate focus should be public safety and the protection of the citizens of Connecticut from those who do not respect them or our laws.

Words cannot express how sad I am that nothing you will do can undo what happened to my family. I write this letter because it is so urgently important that you, as our legislative body, learn from these awful events and take full advantage of this opportunity to comprehensively change our laws to better protect the innocent members of our society.

History has shown us that reputations are made and legacies are established by how the needs of the people are addressed by those responsible for shaping our government's response to tragic events and the crises that follow them. That opportunity exists now for you and our legislature. I strongly urge you to recognize your potential to do significant good, and to seize the opportunity to put aside political differences in order to make our state safer.

I have been told by many, including some elected officials, that our system failed me and my family. You have the responsibility to correct those failures. I respectfully ask that you do everything you can to work cooperatively together, to make full use of your collective talents and energies, and to bring forward meaningful legislative changes that will better protect the safety of our citizens and ensure that past failures are never repeated.

Thank you for your attention to this letter and for your attention to these critically important responsibilities.

Governor Rell, Senator Donald Williams, Representative James A. Amann, Senator John McKinney, and Representative Lawrence F. Cafero, Jr. were all copied on the letter.

Since the Petit murders, Connecticut lawmakers had proposed more than a dozen modifications of the law, including a new law that would make home invasion a "violent crime," and a "three-strikes" law that would impose a mandatory life sentence.

When the Judiciary Committee received Dr. Petit's letter, it was read into the record by Cheshire Representative Al Adinolfi, who lived on Sorghum Mill Drive.

After the reading, Senator John Kissel of the town of Enfield said, "Bricks and mortar aren't going to solve this. We can do a better job of reintegrating the nonviolent offenders into our society, freeing up the beds so that those beds are dedicated to the worst of the worst."

Then there was a taste of the politics that Dr. Petit hoped the body would be able to avoid. Kissel, a Republican, said Democrats were using "scare tactics." He cited a statement by East Haven Representative Michael Lawlor saying that the state universities would have to close if the state was going to come up with enough money to build more prisons.

Lawlor responded, "If we don't put our money where our mouth is, if we don't put the resources out in the field so that the people who are supposed to do this job have the resources they need to actually do it, then it's not going to work."

The governor had set up a task force to work with the Judiciary Committee to come up with further proposals. The Sentencing and Parole Review Task Force was scheduled to report its findings by the end of the year.

On the same day that Dr. Petit wrote his letter, a public hearing was held with Governor Rell's task force. Discussed were possible changes in the way criminals were charged, sentenced, and paroled.

One of the speakers was a woman whose son had been killed by a hit-and-run driver who was high on drugs. When the driver was caught, the mother reported, she learned that the driver had been arrested seven times before but had never been sentenced to prison.

"I was devastated. I felt that our system was responsible also for killing my son, because if I can commit a crime and can keep getting away with it, and getting back on the street, why not keep committing a crime?" she said. "I'm here because I want to stay optimistic, and I want change because the last thing I want is for anyone to go through what [I] and my other son have gone through."

Even as this hearing was going on, about fifty people were protesting, chanting, and holding signs, outside the Whalley Avenue Prison in New Haven. Their claim was that a ban on parole, while geared toward making the public safer, would actually accomplish the opposite, making the streets and prisons more dangerous.

One of the protesters was Owen Kozlovich, who said he was speaking from experience. He had been paroled only a week before after serving time for failure to pay child support.

"I was locked up side by side with violent offenders," he said. "Fifty of us lived on a gymnasium floor with only one corrections officer. When you cram that many people into a room, eventually someone is going to blow their top. The system is broken, and a parole ban is not going to fix it."

The organizer of the protest, Barbara Fair of People Against Injustice, said, "Many nonviolent offenders are behind bars, and that's making them violent. The overcrowding of prisons is lining the pockets of a growing prison industry. Incarceration is now a billion-dollar industry."

Back at the Judiciary Committee, Chief Public Defender Susan Storey testified that she was concerned that some of the legislation being proposed in the wake of the Petit murders was reactionary. She noted that five different three-strikes bills were being considered, and that the state might end up incarcerating "more people than is warranted."

She wondered which of the bills would actually increase public safety and which would simply fill up the prisons to the bursting point with "people of color." Storey noted that

Connecticut already incarcerated a very large percentage of its residents, the fifth-highest percentage in the country.

Then she noted that that prison population was disproportionately African-American and Latino. Connecticut, she said, incarcerated the largest percentage of its black and Latino population in the country, while its incarceration of white inmates was lower than the national average. Although 10 percent of Connecticut's population was non-white, 70 percent of the prison population was non-white. As is true in all states, the prison population was overwhelmingly male.

State Senator John Kissel took exception to Storey's facts and figures, and both Kissel and Storey agreed to "check their sources."

Representative Arthur O'Neill said, "You don't think anyone should be incarcerated."

"That's not true," Storey replied.

Storey was questioned persistently by the members of the committee, but stuck to her guns, saying, "I will oppose a three-strikes law in all cases. I favor judicial discretion."

Representative Mike Lawlor asked if one way to ease prison overcrowding would be to eliminate the roadblocks to releasing more nonviolent prisoners. Storey agreed that it would. She noted that a thousand of Connecticut's 19,000 or so prisoners were scheduled to be released, but were still being held because there was no place for them to go. Laws limited where an ex-con could live. Released prisoners were not allowed to move into public housing, for example.

"It's very hard, once you have a record, to succeed," she said.

Senator Sam Caligiuri, who sponsored one of the three-strikes bills, said that his bill would be just one tool to keep the public safe and would not greatly affect the prison population. He noted that his bill would allow judges to give a life sentence to any criminal who was being convicted of a third violent felony. He noted that, at that moment, there were only 435 ex-cons with two violent felony convictions who were out of prison and living in Connecticut.

New Haven State Representative Toni Walker, after noting that a three-strikes law in the state of Washington failed to lower the crime rate, asked Caligiuri if his bill, had it been enacted a year before, would have prevented the Petit tragedy. Caligiuri admitted that it would not have. Hayes and Komisarjevsky were simply not categorized as violent offenders.

Walker then said, "I'm concerned about what you're doing, and how we're going about it, and what is our objective. My objective is public safety. And my objective is to address ways that are going to make sure that our communities—all communities, not just one or two communities—are safe. Violence is wrong. Violence needs to be addressed. But we also need to talk about guns, and also about violence—not only in the suburbs, but also in the cities."

One change in Connecticut's legal system that everyone agreed upon was that the state needed a full-time parole board, with qualified members educated in criminal justice. Senate President Pro Tem Donald E. Williams Jr. said that such a board would have better reviewed the records of Hayes and Komisarjevsky, including transcripts of Komisarjevsky's 2002 sentencing hearing in which a judge referred to him as a "cold-blooded predator."

"A better-informed parole board might have kept these two men in jail," Senator Williams said.

On January 8, 2008, Governor Rell called a press conference and announced the recommendations of her task force. She said that new laws she was recommending included one that would classify certain burglaries committed when there were people at home as violent crimes, and one that would replace the current parole board system—seven members, all part-time—with a five-member full-time board. Since they were full time, the governor said, they would have the time to do a complete investigation of the background of each potential parolee. She did not recommend a mandatory life sentence for violent offenders with three convictions, but she did urge an increase in the minimum prison sentences for repeat offenders.

When Dr. Petit was informed that Governor Rell's task force had recommended a strengthening of Connecticut's legal system, including a stiffer law for home invasion, he granted his first interview since the tragedy, agreeing to answer questions via phone from *New York Times* reporter Allison Leigh Cowan.

He called the governor's recommendations "a good start toward improving public safety." He then added that "some of these things may not have protected my family even if they were in place." Dr. Petit revealed that the governor had called him and discussed her recommendations before she called a press conference and announced them to the public. He continued, "I realize that none of this will bring my family back, and some of these things may not have protected my family even if they were in place, but it's just amazing how many cracks there are when people looked. I welcome the governor's support for classifying more home burglaries as a violent crime and for strengthening the Board of Paroles." The *Times* pointed out that Dr. Petit had previously referred to the Board of Paroles as a "total failure."

He also said, disagreeing with the governor, that a "properly written three-strikes-you're-out law made common sense."

He continued, "It's almost beyond belief that you could commit a violent crime and be convicted by a jury of your peers, and then get out and commit a second violent crime and be convicted by a jury of your peers, and then commit a third violent crime and be convicted by a jury of your peers and still get out. If you haven't figured it out yet, then you probably won't, and you should not have the right to remain in civilized society."

Reactions were across the board. Criminal defense attorneys Michael Fitzpatrick and Edward Gavin called three-strikes legislation a "knee-jerk reaction."

Samantha Mannion, chairman of the criminal justice department at Housatonic Community College, said, "I don't know how much impact it will have. I do know that people intent on committing a crime believe they're not going to get caught. They're not calculating the potential sentence they'll face if they are caught."

Bridgeport State Attorney Jonathan Benedict called the governor's recommendations "important changes. This is meant as a deterrent. Burglary is a more serious crime that will carry more consequences. Additional funding for new technology will create an information-sharing system among criminal justice agencies that will be a big help. It will allow us to trade information more easily."

On January 21, 2008, *The Hartford Courant* gained access to the police transcripts of the 911 call on the morning of July 23 and subsequent police activity. The police had not wanted to release the transcript at all and had only done so in response to a Freedom of Information request.

Though there had been rumors, with the release of the transcript it was verified for the first time that there had been a five-minute gap between the first 911 call and the order to send police to the Petit residence, and a twenty-six-minute gap between the arrival of the first officer in the vicinity of the Petit house and when law enforcement first entered the home. The five-minute gap was largely due to the fact that several times dispatchers put the caller—Mary Lyons calling from the Bank of America—on hold, and then told her to call back on a different line and give a further description of the odd occurrence at the bank.

Regarding the twenty-six-minute gap, Lieutenant Peter Hall, a police trainer and former SWAT commander, told a television reporter, "It's not like we're sitting around the station with twenty-something SWAT guys ready to go. Our first objective would be to establish a perimeter and to maintain control of that perimeter, and to try to determine who the bad guys are versus the good guys."

The police released the transcript [a copy of which appears in an appendix to this book] in heavily redacted form to protect the identities of those who may be called to testify in the trials of Joshua Komisarjevsky and Steven Hayes.

According to Lieutenant Jay Markella of the Cheshire Police, in addition to identities, some comments had been redacted that "might be used in the case." Markella was asked for further comment regarding the transcript but refused, citing the gag order in effect.

Chapter 17:

The Cheshire Lights

On Sunday, January 6, 2008, the people of the Cheshire community took another step toward healing. They did it by creating, piece by piece, an awesome work of art using the entire town as their canvas. Instead of brush strokes, they used light—luminaries, candles lit inside white paper bags. By the time they were finished, there were 138,000 candles burning simultaneously. The event was called Cheshire's Lights of Hope, and it was estimated that four hundred streets in and around the town were lined with the flickering lights.

In order to accomplish this stunning feat, teamwork was required. The materials had been stockpiled in a warehouse and were handed out to volunteers. Everyone got into the act. When the streets were finished, one group set up their burning candles in a pattern across an open grassy field.

Volunteer teams were each assigned quarter-mile segments of street and highway. Each team was given 250 luminaries to set out along the roadside. Included were Routes 10 and 68, the town's busiest thoroughfares.

Route 10 was successfully lined with luminaries along its entire length, from Interstate 691 to the Hamden line. The sight was so impressive that drivers slowed as they drove between the lines of light—sometimes out of curiosity and wonderment, sometimes out of respect.

Dr. Petit was nearly overwhelmed by the physical manifestation of the community's support. He blinked at the luminescence almost unbelievingly and then spoke to a gathered crowd.

"My faith has been severely challenged," Dr. Petit said. "But you have all pulled me through. You have kept me afloat. I have had some dark days when I feel like I am in a dark place. Everyone has helped me see some of the light."

And, as if the stunning aesthetics of the event were not enough, the Lights of Hope had served a practical purpose as well. It was part of a fund-raising event held by the Connecticut Chapter of the Multiple Sclerosis Society, which raised more than $100,000 for Hayley's Hope and Michaela's Miracle Fund.

Lisa Gerrol, the president of the state MS society, said, "This is a day to reflect on three amazing women and their work to help MS. Through an unthinkable tragedy, Dr. Petit has inspired this community, this state, and this country to help and do their part to make the world a better place to live."

The Lights of Hope event was organized by Don and Jenifer Walsh, who have two small children. Jenifer was diagnosed with MS in 1998. She wanted everyone to know that an event like the Cheshire lights doesn't happen overnight. Preparations had begun back in September.

"I spent a month recruiting block captains, and then each block captain urged their neighbors to each buy ten luminaries for ten dollars." This was not the first luminaria event the Walshes had helped organize. Their first, in 2006, was on a much smaller scale. It involved forty-five homes and raised money for the American Cancer Society's Relay for Life.

Don Walsh commented, "Five months later, we have been resilient. Cheshire can recover. We will never forget, but we can recover. "Do something in your own little way to remember these three remarkable women."

Among those setting out the lights were Sorghum Mill Road resident Michael Savino and his neighbors Nora, Molly, and Mairead Moore, who ranged in age from sixteen to twenty.

"When I realized I needed help, I knew they would help," Savino said. The four-person team set out the lights on Route 68 near Deepwood Drive.

"Since our street was already done, we came over here to make sure West Cheshire was covered as well," said Nora Moore. "We felt because we're in the neighborhood, it was a good way to help."

Though many began during the late morning hours, the work extended past dusk and into the nighttime. Workers were urged to wear Day-Glo safety vests so no one would get hit by a car. Among those wearing the vests were Liz Fiocco and Alicia Martino, both fifteen years old.

"This shows how a community can come together," Martino said.

"It shows healing," added Fiocco.

The congregation of Saint Bridget's Church on Main Street gathered in the parish hall and placed luminaries all around the church property.

"This has made the town strong," said Ron Gizzi of Hamden. "Cheshire is really pulling together for this."

In several places throughout the town, the luminaries were used to spell out the word "Hope." One of those locations was Cheshire Academy. Among those setting out the tiny lights at the academy were Courtney Fox and Joy Nemerson, both thirteen years old, who attended the academy's middle school. They both knew Jennifer and Michaela. About Michaela, Fox said, "She was really easygoing and had a good sense of humor."

Karen Butler of the Greater Hartford Chapter of the MS Society said the luminaria was a truly inspired way to raise money. "It's visual. It illustrates community and unity," she said. "It's fairly inexpensive and just about anybody can be involved. Especially with a compelling story, quite a bit of money can be raised."

About three weeks later on January 27, a second luminaria event called Shining Peace Upon the Petits was held in Dr. Petit's hometown of Plainville. Organized by Lisa Riera, luminaries were placed four feet apart along a seven-mile stretch of Route 10 between Plainville and Plantsville, passing through Plainville. In addition to Route 10, the lights were also placed along Flanders Street in Southington and on Whiting Street in Plainville. In places the lights were used to spell out messages such as "Hope," "Peace on Earth," and the victims' initials.

Riera, a real estate agent who lives in Southington, said she had been inspired by the Lights of Hope ceremony and had wanted to show the solidarity of Cheshire's nearby community. The money raised during the event went to the Petit Family Foundation, which supported various causes including student scholarships and fighting violence against women.

Lisa and her husband Peter spent six weeks organizing the event and put together an army of three hundred volunteers. The volunteers ranged in age from four to eighty-six and included a group from the Plainville Association for Retarded Citizens.

"One of the most important things is that all of the area schools have gotten involved," Lisa Riera said. "That's important because it is kids who need to change the world."

A representative from one of those schools, Cyndi Simms of the Thalberg Parent-Teacher Organization, said, "I don't think there's anybody who doesn't feel for the Petits, but Thalberg School itself has a special connection to the family. It impacted me so deeply that there was no way we couldn't do something."

She noted that some of the Petits' cousins had gone to school at Thalberg, and the family was also related to second-grade teacher Andrea LaChapelle.

"I received donations from children as young as five, dollar bills, it shows me how deeply this affects even kindergarteners. It was very touching to open those envelopes and see their little handwriting," Simms said.

The luminaries were made on a Sunday at Yarde Metals. A total of 25,000 luminaries were made and sold for a dollar apiece. More donations were received through the website set up to support the event, www.shiningpeace.org.

At four in the afternoon on the day of the event, a short prayer service was held in the gazebo at Plantsville Clock Tower Square, with Reverend Victoria Triano presiding. Dr. Petit thanked the gathering for "every candle lit," and the service ended with a singing of *Amazing Grace.*

The event ended at nightfall, a wintry chill in the air, at Veteran's Memorial Park in Plainville, across the street from Dr. Petit's office. William Petit's brother Michael spoke there, quoting the scriptures and reminding those gathered that Christ was the light of the world.

"Bring that light home with you," Michael Petit said. "To your town, to your nation, to the world. We have the ability to change the world, one life at a time." With that a group of teenagers lit the luminaries in the park, spelling the word "Hope."

"I was driving home when I saw the lights," said Andrew Wyzga of Southington. "It was the most awesome thing I've ever seen in my life. They went on for miles and miles. I was moved."

After the lights were laid out, a dinner was held for the volunteers to celebrate the event's success at Southington High School with food donated by local restaurants and brought to the school by the school's National Honor Society students.

Lisa Riera told a reporter for a local newspaper that her event had received contributions from as far away as Michigan and Florida, but her favorite contribution came from a woman in Atlanta, who wrote, "Jennifer, Hayley, and Michaela will look down from Heaven and see the lights."

Chapter 18:

Then It Happened Again

It was early spring 2008, and public anxiety was diminishing in central Connecticut. Folks were able to relax again in their own homes. Some were sleeping better, sleeping all the way through without getting up to make sure all the doors were locked.

Then it happened again.

"It" being a home invasion that turned deadly. This time it was in New Britain, Connecticut, the town where Dr. Petit did his hospital work. Sixty-two-year-old Mary Ellen Welsh, who was battling cancer, was enjoying a Sunday afternoon coffee with her friend, sixty-five-year-old Carol Larese, on Woodhaven Drive when thirty-one-year-old Leslie Williams broke into the house and shot them both.

Williams later said that he intended only to take money and steal a car but was surprised when he encountered the women. He took Larese into the basement, shot her once, and left her for dead. She survived the shot by playing dead and made a full recovery.

Williams kidnapped Welsh in her stolen car. He eventually shot her as well, killing her. He dumped her body in a quarry ten miles away in Bristol. Police arrested Williams later in the day in Watertown after discovering him driving Welsh's stolen car.

Attorney Todd Edgington said, "In some ways this is a repeat of Cheshire. They had just loosened the bonds on the entire prison parole system, and this has the potential to set the whole system back."

Like Komisarjevsky and Hayes, Williams was an ex-con who had been out of prison for only days. He'd served eight years for repeatedly raping a five-year-old girl. In 2006 he had been denied parole when state officials determined it was a near-certainty that he would commit more crimes if set free. During his prison stint he had been disciplined several times for threats, security tampering, and writing inappropriate letters to a female prison counselor.

Of course, unlike Hayes and Komisarjevsky, Williams had a very violent background. Legally, it wasn't a valid comparison. But the people of central Connecticut didn't care much about "legal." They cared about emotional, and the fear Williams had caused was the same as that caused by Hayes and Komisarjevsky. As long as people couldn't feel safe inside their homes, who could relax?

And so central Connecticut was back on edge. In a small tavern in Bristol, not far from where Welsh's body was found, one patron said, "This has changed the way we live forever."

Chapter 19:

More Legislative Debate

As Dean Pagani, former gubernatorial advisor and vice president of public affairs for Cashman and Katz Integrated Communications in Glastonbury, pointed out in March 2008, those who argue for longer prison sentences for repeat offenders such as Komisarjevsky and Hayes are often the same people who, being fiscally conservative, would never approve the money necessary to build the new prisons that such longer sentences would necessitate.

Pagani said:

> *In the unsettling days following the Petit murders, as politicians raced to take action, a kernel of public policy truth emerged during legislative hearings before the Judiciary Committee. Correction Commissioner Theresa Lantz, who is known as an honest and competent professional, told the committee that tougher sentencing laws and expanding prison populations may eventually require the state to build two new prison facilities; one for general population and one for the mentally ill.*
>
> *Within forty-eight hours, her office was forced to clarify that she wasn't proposing new prison construction, she was just thinking out loud that it would appear. The idea of spending about $210 million for the two facilities was also stricken from the public record never to be repeated again. It's unfortunate this line of discussion has been cut off because statistics and our growing understanding of mental illness clearly show that a large percentage of the nation's prison*

population suffers from some form of mental illness. Treating mental illness might have the same positive effects on the system that incarceration alternatives would have on the daily population count.

There are three reasons lawmakers are reluctant to talk about mental health for convicts. The first is expense; the cost of providing health care to inmates is already incredibly expensive. Adding full scale mental-health coverage would drive up the cost further. Second, showing compassion toward prison inmates—never mind spending more money on them—is not politically popular. Three, government spends money on crisis, not prevention.

Because of the gag order and the deliberate pace at which the legal case against Hayes and Komisarjevsky was moving forward, it was very difficult for the media to find anything to report. On March 11, papers in and around Connecticut reported that, on that day, the two defendants had talked with the New Haven state's attorney. "No other details were available," the article said.

On Tuesday, March 12, 2008, Dr. Petit's sister Johanna, flanked by her parents, met with Connecticut legislators and asked that they pass legislation requiring a mandatory life sentence for repeat violent offenders. She read a five-minute statement to the body, which expressed her frustration with the legal system, and then left without answering any questions.

She said, "We understand that the tragedy that befell us last July occurred through randomness, as well as a system that placed the rights of the accused and convicted beyond those of the victims. To date, our legal system has left [Hayes and

Komisarjevsky] in jail for 233 days without any real action occurring."

She thanked the body for the steps already taken—the new home-invasion law making burglary among the list of crimes that could trigger the three-strikes law—but said, "However, there is more that needs to be done. We as a family and my brother as a father and husband have been sentenced to life without his family and without any chance of 'parole.'"

Chief State's Attorney Kevin Kane told legislators there are many defendants who meet the definition of persistent offender but should not face a life sentence. "Under the present law, a defendant who commits two burglaries at age nineteen and then gets into a serious bar fight as a thirty-year-old could be prosecuted as a persistent offender," Kane said. "Sometimes the very essence of justice is discretion. The persistent offender law is useful to prosecutors, even when it is not used; to avoid being charged under the law, defendants often will plea to a more significant charge. It's definitely used during the plea negotiation process."

After the meeting, Johanna expressed frustration: "The three-strikes bill is about those who have offended society in a violent way three times. They just do not get it."

On March, 19, 2008, Dr. Petit's letter to the State Judiciary Committee and the in-person plea by his sister proved insufficient to get that committee to pass the so-called "three-strikes law." By a twenty-five to sixteen vote, the legislation died.

Proponents of the law—largely Republicans—on the committee said that they would keep pushing for a mandatory minimum sentencing bill for dangerous offenders. Opponents—largely Democrats—said that the law was deceiving because it did not automatically require a life sentence for a third violent offense but rather left the matter to the discretion of prosecutors.

According to committee co-chairman, Representative Michael Lawlor, the law, if it had passed, would have been seldom used. "The bottom line is the law is very misleading," he said.

Governor Rell disagreed. "Chairman Lawlor has been saying that for months, frankly, that it doesn't do anything, that it's really a show only," Rell told reporters at the State Capitol. "Well, if that's all it is, then let's pass the bill and make sure that the people get what they're calling for, which is let's get the criminals off the street. And when you have committed three violent felonies, that you are sent to prison for the rest of your life. If he says it doesn't do anything and it really makes no difference, then pass the bill and see if it really does accomplish anything."

The defeated bill had been proposed by Representative Lawrence J. Cafero. In light of the bill's defeat, his words were harsh. "The public now knows that the Democratic lawmakers who thwarted the public outcry over this tragedy also refused to heed the pleas of the family who have repeatedly called for mandatory life sentences for dangerous, repeat criminals," Cafero said.

Although this bill was killed, the same body had passed a law in January 2008 that made it easier for judges to impose a life sentence for third-time offenders. As the effectiveness of that law had yet to be tested, Senator Andrew McDonald commented, "We are trying to fix something that we don't know as yet is broken."

Evil is a word most often used by poets, priests, and philosophers. But it is seldom used by politicians and legislators. Ronald Reagan used it when describing the Soviet Union as the "Evil Empire," and it caused quite a fuss. George W. Bush once referred to North Korea, Iran and Iraq as the "Axis of Evil." On April 1, 2008 Governor Rell used the word to describe criminals whose very nature made rehabilitation impossible.

There were certain criminals, she said, who were evil. Born that way and they'd die that way—and they should be locked away, the key tossed. She made the statement in support of the three-strikes legislation she had proposed, and it prompted an editorial in the *Republican-American* newspaper that said, "The problem becomes identifying such creatures and putting them behind bars forever, before they have had a chance to commit the monstrous crimes programmed into them. That's the concept behind 'three-strikes' legislation proposed by Gov. Rell and legislative Republicans, and resisted mightily by majority Democrats."

Not all legislation was killed. Because of this case, on January 22, 2008, the Connecticut general assembly voted to reform state law. Six months to the day following the attack on the Petits, a new law was passed making it a separate crime to invade a home, a crime that would carry a minimum penalty of ten years in prison.

While the three-strikes debate continued, some Connecticut communities were attempting to protect their children by strengthening restrictions on convicted sex offenders. Bristol—where Joshua Komisarjevsky had lived for a time with his girlfriend—had recently adopted a law that would forbid sex offenders from entering areas likely to be frequented by children, such as playgrounds and public parks.

This law was already in place in Danbury and New Milford and was being considered in Windsor Locks. The State General Assembly was considering a measure that would prohibit sex offenders from living within a thousand feet of schools. *The Stamford Times* printed an editorial by Chris Powell, the managing editor of the *Journal Inquirer*, that called the new laws "silly." Powell believed that, although the new laws might make the public feel safer and make the lawmakers appear as if they were doing something, the laws in actuality were useless.

"If the regular criminal law cannot deter people from kidnapping or raping people or seducing minors, how will a zoning ordinance do better? Are towns going to station police officers at park entrances to demand identification from everyone and delay everyone's admission until each identification has been checked against the state's sex-offender registry?" Powell wrote. "And how much will a law forbidding sex offenders from living within a thousand feet of a school discourage them from getting closer unless cars, buses, bicycles, and shoes are outlawed as well?"

To prove his point he cited a recent rape in Bristol that took place in a public park by a registered sex offender who was wearing an electronic monitoring bracelet. He stated that government in Connecticut was satisfying itself with "imaginary protections" because it simply can't afford real protections. Powell called for an all-out attack on drug crimes in the state and the passing of a mandatory life sentence for third-time offenders law. If that meant new prisons would need to be built, so be it.

It wasn't until the spring of 2008 that the Connecticut state House came up with "three-strikes" legislation that it could agree upon. Reporter Paul Hughes of the *Republican-American* called it a "three-strikes-and-you-might-be-out" bill. The legislation, proposed by Democrats, gave judges the option of sentencing three-time losers to life sentences, but not without the possibility of parole. The bill applied to felonies such as murder, manslaughter, arson, kidnapping, assault, sexual assault, home invasion, robbery, and burglaries. Sentences for second and third convictions would be doubled and tripled, respectively. The bill was voted upon on the nine-month anniversary of the Petit murders and passed by a vote of one hundred twenty-eight to twelve.

Chapter 20:

March Madness: A Turning Point in the Healing Process

March Madness is the common nickname for the NCAA basketball tournament, which over the course of three weeks determines college basketball's national champion. It is a fun source for office pools across the land. In Cheshire a different kind of March Madness came to the basketball court, as a tournament was held on March 15, 2008 to honor the Petit victims and to raise money for the Multiple Sclerosis Society.

The basketball tournament was the idea of Megan Alexander, Hayley's childhood friend—the same young woman who had been misquoted by the *New York Post* about seeing Joshua Komisarjevsky mowing lawns. Megan had started school at Syracuse University the previous fall, majoring in public relations, but had quickly come to the conclusion that it was too early for her to leave home. She needed home. And home needed her. So she made an arrangement with the school to take a leave of absence and study at home for a year, which gave her the opportunity to help her community through the tough time it was having. And vice versa.

"My first thought about the Petits is always the MS Society and all of the work they've done for that. I knew the family when Jen was diagnosed with MS and I walked with Hayley in the MS walk in 2003. So I knew how important it was to them," Megan explained. "And, of course, my second thought was basketball. Hayley Petit loved basketball. When Hayley was really little she was an avid basketball fan and player. And that continued throughout high school. By the end of high school she had become mostly a rower for crew. That was what she wanted to do in college, but I had originally known her as a basketball player and that was how I always thought of her," Megan said. "Hayley always used to joke around that she was going to play hoops for the UConn women when she grew up. It was a big part of their family life. Dr. Petit always took her to games and it was always on the TV at their house. I wanted to combine the family's two loves and do something they would be proud of. When I was trying to think of something that would both raise money and that people would enjoy, basketball obviously came to my mind. This is celebrating what they had fun doing, because they were a really fun family."

So Megan and three of her friends—Justin Ivey, Steve Selnick, and Wayne Lawrence—went to work and organized the first annual Dunk it: Petit Family Memorial Basketball Tournament. Justin, a Cheshire High School senior, said, "The Petits donated a lot to their community. Their family would have raised the money, so doing it in their name means a lot."

Thirty-six teams of basketball players, all sponsored by generous supporters and ranging in age from eight to sixty-five, swished and dished from Saturday morning to Saturday night in the Cheshire High School gym. Team check-in began at 9:30 at the boys' gym in the high school. Opening ceremonies were held at 10:00 a.m. in the Thorpe Auditorium. At 11:00 a.m. was the first tip-off. At 4:00 p.m. there was a break for a full-court game between the Cheshire Police Department and Wallingford Police Department in the boys' gym.

Admission to the event was free but it cost $15 to play. There was also a donations table set up to take any amount of money from anyone who wanted to give it. More than $10,000 was raised for the National Multiple Sclerosis Society and the Hayley's Hope and Michaela's Miracle MS Memorial funds.

A team from Ferrazzi Limousines won the adult league. Some teams were named after their sponsors. Others had funny names that were take-offs on the sponsors' wares—like the Doughballers, who were sponsored by a pizza place.

Dr. Petit was the guest of honor and sat courtside through-out. At one point, when a ball came bouncing his way, Dr. Petit caught it and decided to take a shot at the basket. It didn't go in but the crowd went wild cheering and the doctor smiled. It was the first time anyone had seen him smile since . . . well, just since.

Dr. Petit later told a reporter, "This is a wonderful event because it's spearheaded by one of Hayley's close friends, Megan Alexander, and her three friends, Justin, Wayne, and Steve. But it's hard sometimes, because it's a good thing, but you wish you weren't here."

One of the hoopsters—Jamie Erickson, a sophomore at Cheshire High School—said that he also planned to walk in the MS Walk-a-thon in May. About that walk he said, "Hayley participated in it for seven years and Michaela was supposed to take her place, and me and two friends—Elizabeth and Kath-erine Thompson—decided to make a team called the Precious Petits and organize members to walk."

Weeks later, looking back on the success of the tournament, Megan Alexander believed that the basketball tournament rep-resented a new stage in the community's healing process. Up until that time, all of the events for the Petits had been sol-emn. This was the first occasion during which people could remember and pay tribute, and have fun at the same time. Now enough light had been created by the caring people of central Connecticut that smiles were returning to their faces.

"Obviously I have a lot of respect for all of the things people had done before, but I thought it was time to do something a little different," Megan explained. "The feeling was really positive that day. It was the first community event that I had been to where people were smiling and having fun with their families and friends. Sure there were moments of remembrance, but the focus was more on looking toward the future."

Megan believed that they were healing as a community far better than they would have as individuals. "Right from the memorial service, through the candlelight vigil, and the luminaria, the community events have represented where we are in our healing process, and the basketball tournament represented a major step forward," she said. "There are people online who think that there have been too many ceremonies and too many remembrances, that it would be better to just leave Dr. Petit alone. But I think our community has needed the excuses to get together. The people who think it has been too much aren't the people living here and they aren't the people who have been talking to Dr. Petit."

And the event, organized and run entirely by teenagers, is destined to become an annual event. "Since we're all going to be away at school next year, my mom, Deb Hereld, is going to take it over," Megan explained.

Megan says that, of course, everyone would give anything to get the Petit women back, but the tragedy has had a positive influence on the town of Cheshire. "There is a sense of community here now that wasn't here before," Megan said during the spring of 2008. "I never thought of us as a tight-knit community before. We had the Relay for Life. That was huge here and it's great. But the number of community events that have happened here this year has just been incredible."

In the spring of 2008 the Petit Family Foundation, the same organization that had held the golf tournament the previous fall, was busy planning a 5K run to raise money. The race was scheduled for July 20, 2008, very close to the first anniversary of the tragedy. Advertisements for the run urging donors to sponsor runners featured the foundation's new slogan: "Be the Change." The slogan is a reference to the Mahatma Gandhi quote—"you must be the change you wish to see in the world"— that Michaela embraced and put on her Facebook page.

The day would also feature a Kids' Fun Run, and for those who didn't run, a 5K Fitness Walk. The 5K course would be in Plainville where Dr Petit grew up and practiced medicine, starting on Route 10, heading south in front of the McDonald's and finishing on Woodford Avenue in front of the Plainville General Electric facility. After the race there would be music and refreshments, an awards ceremony, and a raffle.

A corner, indeed, had been turned—and the road ahead looked bright. Much money was still being raised for the charities that the Petits held dear, but the nights of candlelight vigils were over, having been replaced by golf, basketball, and "Fun Runs."

Chapter 21:

The Grieving Schools: Miss Porter's, Chase Collegiate, and Cheshire Academy

Among the places most profoundly affected by the murders were the schools attended by Hayley and Michaela, Miss Porter's School and Chase Collegiate School, respectively, and the school where Jennifer worked, Cheshire Academy.

Miss Porter's School, the high school from which Hayley had graduated only a few weeks before her death, was twenty-two miles from the Petit home, making for quite a commute. There were boardinghouses at the school, but Hayley continued to live at home while she attended the school.

Founded by Sarah Porter in 1843, Miss Porter's was considered one of the finest all-girl high schools in the world. Tuition was $40,440 a year. Among its graduates were Jacqueline Bouvier Kennedy Onassis and Helen Coley Nauts, the founder of the Cancer Research Institute.

The head of the school for the past fifteen years had been sixty-seven-year-old Mrs. A. Burch Tracy Ford. She and her family had been living in boarding schools for thirty-four years. Before Miss Porter's, she worked at the Milton Academy, where she taught psychology and was the dean of students; the Groton School for ten years, where she taught psychology and ethics and was the school counselor; and the Concord Academy, where her husband taught and she ran a dorm while doing graduate work. In terms of being an educator, she felt her most formative experience was her two years in the Peace Corps in Senegal in West Africa. She earned her bachelor's degree at Boston University, her master's in clinical social work at Simmons College, and a second master's in educational management at Harvard.

Remembering Hayley, Mrs. Ford said, "Hayley was such a good, good person. The younger kids just worshipped the ground she walked on. She was gentle and reserved. She didn't tell anyone that she had been accepted early at Dartmouth. If you learned about her accomplishments or the awards she had won, it was because someone else told you. Here was a girl who was on TV receiving an award and yet she would never call attention to herself. That was one of her most remarkable characteristics. And how many students raise tens of thousands of dollars for medical research? That was the reason she was so well loved, because she was so interested in everyone else. Kids not only wanted to be with her, they wanted to *be* her. They didn't just like her, they wanted to *be* like her."

Mrs. Ford had traveled to Asia on business after the 2007 graduation ceremonies. When her business was concluded, she went to India and visited the Taj Mahal. She returned home on Monday, July 23, and immediately heard the horrible news. She recalled:

> *We came through the door at about 10:30 in the morning and the phone was ringing. It was the mother of one of my advisees. Hayley was one of my advisees as well. This was the mother of one of her very closest friends. Her daughter had just called her in terrible distress. We were just stunned. My husband knew Hayley well also. He teaches at another school, but he was Hayley's crew coach, and she was captain.*

A short time later I got another call from a mother who told me that many of Hayley's classmates would be gathering at their house that afternoon, and she asked if I wanted to come over. So I did and it was just crushing. Parents and kids were just distraught. It was incomprehensible. I know it could happen to anyone, but that it happened to the Petits—one of the kindest and most service-oriented families, totally unself-absorbed, always interested in the people around them and in service, and in helping people in any number of ways—made it even more painful.

There is always the assumption, I think, that goodness will protect you—but here was proof that it wasn't so, and it terrified all of the families. Fathers felt terrified that they couldn't protect their families. Children were sleeping with their parents.

Even before the murders, Mrs. Ford had tried to modernize the school curriculum to better prepare her students for harsh realities, but she knew there were no classroom lessons that could prepare her students for a tragedy of this magnitude. Mrs. Ford appointed herself the unofficial school grief counselor. She made herself available to every student, both current students and classmates of Hayley who were going away to college, and talked about their feelings.

"I told them that their highly emotional response was normal," she explained. Mrs. Ford put herself on call for any student who needed to talk, night or day. "I urged them to express their grief in personal ways. We explained that there was no right way or wrong way to grieve and we had to respect one another however we chose to do that. The students were really quite wonderful—as they always are." She continued having individual and group sessions with students throughout the summer.

On Tuesday morning, July 24, only twenty-four hours after the attack, Dr. Petit was receiving visitors, and the Fords went to see him in the hospital.

"We didn't even know if he would be conscious, but he was, and he was lucid. He told me then that he wanted to establish a scholarship in Hayley's name at Miss Porter's," Mrs. Ford remembered. As of April 2008, more than $75,000 had been raised for that scholarship fund.

When school started, Mrs. Ford scheduled the service in memory of the Petits for the end of September, rather than the first week of school.

"We didn't want to open the school year with it. We wanted to orient all of the new students who were starting at Miss Porter's before the service, plus we wanted to give Hayley's best friends, who were college freshmen, an opportunity to come back and attend the service. They, too, by that time would have had a chance to establish a new routine. It would have made their leaving and starting a new life at college that much more painful if we'd had it right at the beginning of school," Mrs. Ford said.

The night before the service the school held a grief counseling meeting for parents. Mrs. Ford invited Dr. Petit to come to the school and speak to the students. Dr. Petit brought bouquets of flowers for Hayley's basketball teammates.

"We had a beautiful service, with talks given by a number of us, including Hayley's closest friends. Her father spoke once again, and he was amazing—absolutely heroic. We held a reception, and there were more than five hundred people there. Of course, there was still an overwhelming sadness, but by the time people were leaving, the closeness they felt to one another was already incredibly healing," Mrs. Ford said. "As the year went on, and it has been a good year, Hayley's name would frequently come up. If there was a particular problem or a dilemma, a student would ask, 'What would Hayley do?' We talked about one of the ways we can keep Hayley with us is to emulate her."

A 2005 graduate of the school who had been Hayley's teammate in crew, Jordan E. Dudek, was amazed at the job Mrs. Ford was doing with the girls. "It takes a special place to allow so many people to gather and comfort each other after something this tragic and life changing," Jordan explained. "Mrs. Ford has helped to maintain that type of community. Even though she was extremely upset about what happened, she was able to give so much of herself to everyone else and provide an environment in which everyone could grieve and comfort each other."

Dr. Barbara Greenspan, a Connecticut psychologist who volunteered to help the school *pro bono*, was also amazed by Mrs. Ford's strength. "I walked out of Miss Porter's School marveling that Mrs. Ford was carrying all of these girls on her shoulders," Dr. Greenspan said.

Asked if there were any experiences in her background that prepared her for grief management on this scale, Mrs. Ford said, "On one level all counseling therapy is about grief. What troubles most of us is loss of some kind or another. But this is so out of the ordinary that I don't know if there is any preparation for something as horrifying and tragic as this event, in its enormity and sadism, and in the goodness of the people involved. This is just on a different scale."

During the spring of 2008 events in Hayley's honor were still being held. The school rowing team held races against Farmington High School for what was now called Hayley's Cup.

As the 2007–2008 school year progressed, Mrs. Ford noticed a change in her girls. The campus was peaceful. She noticed "fewer crises over inconsequential matters. Everybody had seen what real loss was."

The Chase Collegiate School, where both Hayley and Michaela attended grade school, was in the town of Waterbury. Like Miss Porter's School, Chase Collegiate could trace its roots back to the middle of the nineteenth century. It was founded in 1865—the year the Civil War ended and Abraham Lincoln was assassinated—when it was known as Collegiate Institute.

The original school closed in 1874 and reopened a year later as St. Margaret's School for Girls, an Episcopalian school named after the Scottish Queen Margaret. From 1912 through the mid-1970s, St. Margaret's functioned as the sister school to an all-boys school called the McTernan School. At that time the two schools merged and became a nondenominational and coeducational school called St. Margaret's-McTernan School.

In 2005 the school was renamed Chase Collegiate because the use of "St. Margaret" in the name of a nondenominational school was misleading. The school taught children from pre-kindergarten through twelfth grade. There were approximately five hundred students in all, and sixty-seven faculty members. The campus was built on forty-seven acres of land and children came from all over Connecticut to attend.

One girl in Michaela's class said she would never forget the last day of school in June 2007. It was the last day of fifth grade, and the class was moving up to the middle school that fall. She said, "We were taking our last steps out of the lower school building, and we said goodbye to everybody. And I always think, when I said goodbye to Michaela for the summer it was really goodbye forever."

"It feels as though it's not real, like it's just a big bad dream we are all going to wake up from," said one middle-schooler.

"The students found her just the glue of the class; everyone liked her," said Chase Collegiate headmaster John Fixx. "Everyone wanted to be around her. So her loss has been very difficult for the class."

The school held a ceremony in September not long after the students returned. Three weeping cherry trees were planted on the school grounds in memory of the Petits who had died.

"We wrote letters to her and planted them in with the trees when we filled them, so there are words with her, underneath with her," said one student who had been a friend of Michaela's.

Dr. Petit called the school and announced his intention to establish a scholarship fund in his youngest daughter's name, the Michaela Rose Petit '14 Scholarship Fund.

To raise money for the fund, the head of the Chase Collegiate Middle School, John Carpenter, a man who had never met Michaela (she had been scheduled to begin attending the middle school that autumn), decided to dedicate his run in the November 4, 2007 New York City Marathon to the cause. Though he had only started at Chase in September, he founded Miles for Michaela so that people could pledge whatever they could per mile that he ran.

Even though Carpenter had not known Michaela, he was taking over a school filled with students who missed her very much. "It was such a surreal and traumatic event, just feeling that palpable sense of shock and grief," Carpenter said. The cherry trees had been a good start, but he sensed that his students needed more. "For a lot of her classmates, they weren't comfortable using her name. They would pass by the tree every day but I just sensed that they were looking for a sign or signal to acknowledge her absence. I would go out for runs and hear Dr. Petit's words about moving forward—and running is literally moving forward, putting one foot in front of the other as fast as you can. And so the idea just kind of, was born on one of those evening runs."

He set up a Miles for Michaela website, with a photo of Michaela and Hayley, and another of Michaela with her mother. Carpenter said he was also running in honor of Jennifer Hawke-Petit, who had been enormously dedicated to the Chase Collegiate School's Health & Wellness Program. According to the Miles for Michaela website, Jennifer "spearheaded the initiative to encourage healthy lifestyles throughout Chase's fifteen levels."

Dr. Petit was deeply moved by Carpenter's efforts. When he heard of Carpenter's intentions, Dr. Petit said, "I hope everyone will honor my beautiful family by helping a neighbor, fighting for a cause, and loving your family. John Carpenter will have blisters after the marathon but they will be blisters of devotion, and I admire him for that, and I thank him for that."

When it came to race day, Dr. Petit went to New York with his parents and his nephew Andrew, stood at the twenty-mile mark of the 26.2-mile race, and congratulated Carpenter as he went past. Carpenter paused long enough to have his photo taken with Dr. Petit and then was on his way—as his fans cheered in unison "See John run! See John run!"—earning more money for the scholarship fund with every mile he completed.

When the race was over and the math was done, Carpenter was proud to say he raised $8,554 for his day's work. Later, Carpenter claimed that completing the 26.2 miles was easier because running for a good cause helped him get through the ordeal. He finished the entire course in a time of four hours, nineteen minutes, and thirteen seconds.

Just because the marathon was over, that didn't mean the end for Miles for Michaela. Carpenter posted a notice on his website, milesformichaela.org, saying that any run could support the cause. If a runner wanted to join forces, he or she simply had to notify Miles for Michaela and they would help the individual promote their effort and attract a maximum number of sponsors.

Jennifer's place of employment, the Cheshire Academy, which was only a few hundred yards from the Super Stop & Shop, was even older than either Miss Porter's or Chase. It could trace its history to 1794, when it was founded by Samuel Seabury as the Episcopal Academy of Connecticut. By the nineteenth century, the school became known informally as the Cheshire Academy, but the name change was not made official until the early 1900s. It served as a prep school for careers in the military during its first 120 years. In 1917 it revamped its curriculum for students preparing to enter Yale. The school underwent a major expansion on the occasion of its bicentennial celebration.

Jennifer had been co-director of the school's health center. Since the school had boarders, she often used tender loving care to treat homesickness as well as physical ailments.

Right after the murders, the school's director of communications, Philip Moore, became the spokesman who handled reporters. He said, "It's a very difficult day here. Jennifer was very good at educating kids about good health, not just taking care of them when they are not feeling well. We have about four hundred students here. We sent out e-mails today to the parents of every student.

"We're an international school, so a lot of our kids are literally in other countries right now. We wish there wasn't a separation. While we are geographically distant, we are emotionally close. We will have grief counselors available. We are planning a memorial service in the fall when students return to school."

A month later Moore said that he was aware that not all of his students would be recovering from their shock and dealing with their grief at the same rate. "We have to be careful where people are," he said. "It's a difficult line to walk with that grave of a situation. The convocation on September 5 [when students started classes for the new year] will not focus on Jennifer."

"The memorial service in her honor will be held on September 8," said Barbara Dupre, who was coordinating the service for the school. "The public will not be invited, although we do plan on inviting members of the Cheshire police and fire departments to attend."

By the end of August, the Jennifer Hawke-Petit Scholarship Fund had surpassed $23,000. By April 2008, that figure was up to $43,000. According to the scholarship's page on the academy's website, the scholarship was established "to provide talented, socially conscious young women with the opportunity to lead lives of promise and to make their own great contributions to the betterment of society."

Chapter 22:

Forever Michaela

Elizabeth Ollero was a close friend of Michaela's. Even though months had gone by, she still found herself thinking about Michaela all the time.

"I think about her every day. Things will happen and I'll be like, 'Oh, I remember when me and Michaela did that,'" Elizabeth recalled.

With the New Year, Elizabeth decided that she had to find a way to channel her grief, to *do* something to honor her friend. She came upon the idea of creating a website, and that's how forevermichaela.com was born.

"Well, actually, it started at my birthday party," Elizabeth explained. "For my birthday, my friends and I recorded a song. But we didn't know what to do with it. We all wanted to sell it, and my mom said we should donate the money in honor of Michaela. So I came up with donating to the Animal Rescue Site because a few days before Michaela died, she had sent me and some other people a link to the site telling everyone to donate. My mom helped me set it up. She built part of the site, but I came up with the details. My whole family helped me by giving me ideas, especially my sister, my dad, and my mom."

Elizabeth had a few pictures of Michaela—summertime photos, in backyards just out of the pool, relaxing on a couch, hanging out with friends, always flashing that smile full of braces. She even acquired a picture of Michaela when she was a baby, being held by her dad, with older sister Hayley, then about seven years old, standing nearby. The website included a blog where friends and strangers alike could discuss all things Michaela. The website urged visitors to give money to Animal Rescue, MS, and other causes.

The website had not been online for long before it got national attention. Elizabeth explained how it happened.

"We were going to see a show for Kids Night on Broadway, and it was my mom's idea to go to *Good Morning America*. They e-mailed us with our tickets and it said we could bring signs," she said. "My mom told me I could make a sign and I decided I would put the website address on it . . . and hi to my sister and Dad, too. I went with my mom, my friend Lauren Nolan, and her mom, Charlene Nolan."

It was February 5, a dreary, drizzly day as they drove to Times Square and the studios of ABC's *Good Morning America*.

As the show went on—the guests that day were Lenny Kravitz and Vince Vaughn—Elizabeth tried to hold her sign up so that it could be seen on TV.

"We had to wait about a half an hour to get into the building, then an hour until the show went on, and then the show was about two hours. We were there about four or five hours. Well, at first we were in the back holding up our sign because a family didn't want to let us up front. But this lady we met—I forget her name—talked to the people working at *Good Morning America* and she got us up front," Elizabeth recalled. Bottom line: Mission accomplished. Millions of people watching at home saw the little girl holding the sign that invited them to visit forevermichaela.com.

On the way home Elizabeth had her doubts about how successful she had been.

"I knew we were barely on TV, so I was only expecting my family and their friends to see," Elizabeth admitted.

Wrong. When she got home she found that the website was being visited frequently. By the end of the night more than four thousand people had visited the site.

"I was ecstatic!" she said. "I want people to know that Michaela was a really great person and to please not forget about her. It's not fair to Michaela if we only remember her for the bad thing that happened and not the good things."

Elizabeth found that the website made her feel better in a couple of ways. For one thing she was helping to raise money for important charities—as of spring 2008 she had raised $3,000 for MS, and $400 for Animal Rescue—and, for another, the website had given her the freedom to talk about her feelings, to discuss her sadness and grief, things that she had kept bottled up inside of her before.

Elizabeth's positive experiences with community service have led her to branch out. "Besides my stuff for Michaela, I am a member of a group at school called Kids in the Middle for middle-school kids who want to help out at school and volunteer in the community. I enjoy helping people. It makes me feel good to know that I'm doing something good," Elizabeth said.

"I feel as if I'm picking up where she left off and carrying on," Elizabeth said, "And almost making it stronger." In addition to the website, Elizabeth also put together an eighteen-member walk-a-thon team for the May 2008 MS event.

Elizabeth's mother Dayna said, "Elizabeth is now able to talk about Michaela without feeling sad. It's fun for her. It's almost like something she's still doing with Michaela. I'm very proud of her for finding a way to remember Michaela. A lot of the other kids won't even talk or think about her but Elizabeth has turned her memories into a memorial that makes her smile and sometimes even laugh when remembering Michaela."

Obviously, in addition to her own grief, Dayna was very worried about her daughter. Dayna explained, "When we first found out, Chase [Collegiate School] immediately set up a session with teachers and the school counselor. The kids were able to get together at the school to talk to them and to each other and they also had a counselor available for the parents."

What advice would Dayna have for other mothers of children who are dealing with grief? "I think that parents should remember that when someone your child loves dies, it's okay to talk about that person, it's okay to remember them," Dayna explained. " I told Elizabeth that it was okay to be sad and to cry but also that it was okay to talk about Michaela and to remember the fun things they did together. I contacted teachers that Elizabeth was close to so she would have someone to talk to other than just me and her father. Most importantly, just be there for them—if they want to talk and even if they don't."

Afterword:

The Darkness and the Light

Through the spring of 2008, the Petit house was an empty hulk with the windows boarded up. Signs, both on the Hotchkiss Ridge side and on the garage door, read, "Posted. No Trespassing. Keep Out." Above the front door and up the side of the house was a scorch mark from the flames and black smoke that once licked there. Flowers had been tied to a tree on the front lawn with large ribbons. At the corner of the front yard, where Sorghum Mill met Hotchkiss, there was a carefully crafted rock garden with a statue of the Virgin Mary perched on top, and flowers had been left there as well. A large section of the backyard was protected from view by a blue plastic tent. When someone was working there, the front door was left propped open to let air in. The view inside the house from the street revealed only the pitch black of a starless and dreamless night. And yet, in Cheshire and Plainville and the rest of central Connecticut, the lights shined on. . . .

On the morning of May 28, after Dr. Petit visited 300 Sorghum Mill one last time to pick up a few belongings, the Petit home was razed. It shuddered to the ground with a shocking suddenness, and the rest of the day was spent picking up the debris with a backhoe. Many of the trees and shrubs from the property were carefully removed and transported to Plainville, where they became part of a memorial garden. The tree with the large ribbons tied to it was left standing.

Dr. Petit, living with relatives in Plainville, still gets boxes and boxes of mail, 99.9 percent of it supportive. He reads it all and does his best to acknowledge everyone, but it's too much. One wonders if, in his never-ending grief, he realizes the illuminating impact his heroic words have had on his community. Among the thousands of lights, Dr. Petit shines brightest.

Appendix A:

911 Transcript

Note: The released version of the 911 call was heavily redacted.

Dispatcher: Cheshire Emergency.

Caller: [redacted]

Dispatcher: Okay.

Caller: [redacted]

Dispatcher: Okay. Hey can you get [redacted] up here. [Voice in background inaudible.]

Caller: [Redacted]

Dispatcher: Okay. I need you to stay on the line for me, okay?

Officer in background: What do you got?

Dispatcher: Okay ma'am, I'm going to put you on hold, okay?

Caller: [redacted]

[Dial tone.]

Dispatcher: U.U.P. How do I unpark that? [Phone in background, beep, beep.] Ma'am? A-8. Will you seven the desk please ASAP?

Caller: [redacted]

Officer: Roger.

Dispatcher: Okay. Okay, ma'am, I'm going to put you back on hold, all right?

Caller: [redacted]

Dispatcher: HQ to all units.

Officers: One, three.

Dispatcher: HQ to all units. Just got a call from the [redacted] at Bank of America. She stated that [redacted].

Officers: One roger, two roger. C-3.

Dispatcher: Go ahead.

Officer: Higgins Road, just passing Oak. What was the number on Sorghum?

Dispatcher: 300 Sorghum Mill Road. Three, zero, zero. [Voice in background can be heard saying "West Main Street."] HQ to all units, there will be a [redacted].

Officer: Unit 1 copy. I'm turning onto Higgins from South Main now.

Officer: C-3 to Adam 8.

Dispatcher: Copy that.

Officer: Country Club.

Officer: C-3 to C-4.

Officer: A-1 to units. I do not want you to approach the house. Uh, hang back from that location. A-1 to any DB unit on the air.

Caller: [redacted]

Dispatcher: The plate on that vehicle is [redacted].

[Next five spoken statements redacted.]

Officer: A-1 to D-1.

Officer: Go ahead.

Dispatcher: [redacted]

Voices in the background: A-1 to D-1. Go ahead. D-1, did you hear what's been going on the air? Roger, we are in route.

Dispatcher: Did anyone get the license plate? I'm going to have to put you on hold for a couple of minutes, okay?

Caller: [redacted]

Officer: Roger, I'm having a marked unit stay back from, uh, the two-nine. Are you planning on, uh, doing a drive-by of the residence?

Officer: That's a roger.

Officer: Uh, we're gearing up now; we're heading out, we're all unmarked.

Officer: Roger. Uh, we do have a Petit at that location. Uh, however no in house on that, uh, two-nine.

Officer: Roger.

Officer: C-3, somebody grab me my SRT gear.

Officer: Unit 3 to Charlie 3, I'll get your gear out of the locker.

Officer: C-3 to one.

Officer: Unit 1, I'm at the AT&T Tower.

Officer: I'm Sorghum at Hotchkiss on foot trying to stay out of sight.

Officer: That's a roger.

Officer: Unit 3 to A-8.

Officer: Go ahead.

Officer: Do you want me to grab your bag?

Officer: Roger.

Officer: Roger.

Voices in background: HQ, open the south door.

Dispatcher: HQ to all units. I just got a call back from the bank, [redacted].

Officer: A-4 to D-1.

Officer: D-1.

Officer: I'm gonna go to the bank and, uh, meet with the complainant, roger?

Voice in background: Okay.

Officer: Roger.

Officer: A-9 to D-1.

Dispatcher: Ma'am?

Caller: [redacted]

Dispatcher: You said [redacted].

Caller: [redacted]

Officer: Go ahead, A-9.

Voice in background: I'm in the area in my personal vehicle. Do you want me to drive by?

Dispatcher: We're going to have a detective on the way to the bank, okay?

Caller: [redacted]

Voice in background: Roger. Uh, I don't know who I have for patrol. Let's close off both sides of Sorghum.

Officer: C-3 to A-9.

Officer: Roger. A-9 to Unit 1, what's your two-nine?

Officer: C-3 to A-9.

Officer: D-1 to C-3, go ahead.

Officer: I'm just trying to get a visual on the house. I, I cannot see house numbers, so when someone drives by, have them give me the house color and just a quick description, so I can, you know, see if, when these eighteens pull up.

Officer: HQ, you copy.

Officer: Also I need two units over at the Bank of America to [redacted].

Officer: Adam 9 to Charlie 3.

Officer: Go ahead.

Officer: I am on Sorghum. I'm approaching. I'll give you that info in a second.

Officer: Roger. I'm two or three houses past Hotchkiss where my vehicle is parked. I'm just not sure which one is 300. The closest number I had in good view is 260.

Officer: A-4 to D-1, I'm out at the bank.

Officer: Unit 3 to Charlie 3.

Officer: Go.

Officer: Do you need anything else besides your rifle and, uh, your bag and your vest out of here?

Officer: My helmet should be there also.

Dispatcher: Tell the [redacted] that she can [redacted].

Officer: A-2 to 1.

Officer: Unit 1 I'm on Mountain Road, approaching Sorghum.

Officer: Adam 9 to Charlie 3.

Voice in background: Okay, roger.

Officer: A-2 to Unit 2, what's your two-nine?

Officer: Two, I'm on, uh, Higgins by Sorghum.

Officer: Roger. Can you take a position there, and Unit 1 take a position on Sorghum at, uh, Nutmeg?

Officer: Unit 2 copies.

Officer: Adam 9 to Charlie 3.

Officer: Go ahead A-9.

Officer: Okay, the front of the house faces Hotchkiss Ridge. It's a beige colored house. The vehicle in question is in the driveway. Also in the driveway is a [redacted] and I believe the plate is [redacted]. It might be [redacted]. It's a [redacted] and the other vehicle. The [redacted] is in the driveway. The driveway does come out onto Sorghum.

Officer: Okay. I've got a visual on the house it looks like. There's a white and a beige vehicle, roger.

Officer: Right. The [redacted] has a, uh, a badge on the back, Connecticut one hundred club, house has gray shutters. I'm sorry, green shutters and green doors.

Officer: Roger.

Officer: C-3 to HQ.

Officer: Go ahead.

Officer: I suggest that you have some SRT personnel [redacted].

Dispatcher: Roger.

Officer: Unit 1 to Adam 8 [echo] Burrage at Sorghum Mill.

Officer: Adam 8 to Officer Wright.

Officer: Go ahead.

Officer: If you're still at HQ, grab my helmet and, uh, tactical vest.

Officer: Roger. You want the van fired up?

Officer: Roger.

Officer: D-1, I'm seventy.

Dispatcher: Roger, Delta 1. HQ to A-9, did you have a seventeen from the vehicle in question?

Officer: D-1 to Unit 2.

Officer: Unit 2's on.

Officer: Come up to Sorghum and Hotchkiss. [redacted]

Officer: Unit 2 copies.

Officer: D-5 to D-1.

Officer: Go ahead, Joe.

Officer: After you do your drive-by, can we meet you?

Officer: Roger. I will meet you at Sorghum Mill and Sorghum Ridge.

Officer: Roger.

Officer: A-4 to D-1.

Officer: Go ahead.

Officer: Can you give me your cell?

Officer: Roger. It's going to be [redacted]. Who is at the bank?

Officer: Okay.

Dispatcher: HQ to A-4, two-nine?

Officer: A-8 to D-2, correction D-1.

Officer: He's on the seven.

Officer: Unit 3 to A-8.

Officer: Go ahead.

Officer: Where do I meet you?

Officer: Come in from Mountain Road side and I'm up the intersection of, uh, Sorghum Mill and Burrage.

Officer: Roger. Is Charlie 3 at your two-nine?

Officer: Negative.

Officer: Roger.

Officer: Do you have the SRT van?

Officer: Negative.

Officer: C-3 to A-8.

Officer: Go ahead.

Officer: We have two SRT officers on, uh, EDJ, right now.

Officer: Are they with you?

Officer: Negative, but, uh, they're still at their posts right now. I just wanted to let you know that.

Dispatcher: HQ to Adam 4.

[Dial tone and phone ringing in background with unintelligible voices and throat clearing.]

[redacted]

Officer: This is, uh, 91 [911?] operator. Is she speaking with the police right now?

Linda: [redacted]

Officer: C-3 to HQ.

Dispatcher: Go ahead.

Officer: Just be advised at this time I have only a visual on the rear of the house [phone beeping] and the driveway of the house, the front side and the side with the marked units, I don't [phone beeping in background]. . .

Dispatcher: Roger.

Officer: [redacted]

Dispatcher: [redacted]

Officer: Yeah.

Dispatcher: All right. I'm just making sure someone's over there.

Officer: Yeah, I'm over here at the bank. I'm with, uh, with [redacted] and [redacted]. Who's this?

Officer: [redacted]

Officer: Oh, okay. Yeah, we're all set here. I just got off the phone with [redacted]. [In background: Roger.] I relayed all the information to him so he's running with it.

Officer: Okay.

Officer: I just don't want to put too much on the air because, uh, here's what I got just so you know.

Officer: Okay.

Officer: A-8 to A-4.

[Background radio noise.]

Officer: Uh, is someone calling me?

Dispatcher: Yeah, A-8 is.

Officer: A-4 to A-8. Go.

Officer: Do we have any suspect descriptions or anything right now?

Officer: Roger. Roger. It's a [redacted]. Nothing further at this time. I was on the phone with D-1 and he is running with it.

Dispatcher: All right, Jim.

Officer: Did you get that so far?

Dispatcher: Yeah.

Officer: All right. Uh uh, apparently [redacted]

Officer: A-1 to D-1.

Officer: [redacted]

Dispatcher: Okay.

Officer: Go ahead.

Officer: Uh, I have two phone numbers. Uh, let me know when and if you want to make contact with the house. Also I have Trooper One [helicopter] on hold, uh, willing to go up in the air just in case the vehicle leaves the residence.

Officer: Roger. I want to get a perimeter set up and then [redacted].

Officer: Roger, do you want us to make the seven from here or are you going to?

Officer: Okay, and, uh, when, if you get anybody free there, I'm going to need some statements over here. If not we can get them a little bit later, okay?

Officer: Let's get this perimeter set up.

Officer: Roger. Uh, be advised, I am going to make contact, uh, get Trooper One in the air just in case.

Officer: Okay. Yep. That's it. If you need me I'm here at the bank. Just call me on the air.

Dispatcher: All right, do you know [redacted]?

Officer: [in background] Just give me one second. I have a lot of people talking here.

Officer: What's that?

Dispatcher: Did they say [redacted]?

Officer: [redacted]

Dispatcher: Okay. All right.

Officer: Okay, I'll get more as I get it.

Dispatcher: Okay.

Officer: A-8 to D-1.

Officer: Go ahead.

Officer: I have three patrol units at Sorghum Mill—Sorghum Mill and Burrage. Where would you like us or do you want us all to maintain a position here?

Officer: The first entrance, which will be the south entrance to Sorghum at Hotchkiss Ridge. I want at least two cars and, uh, we have two unmarked cars in the area right now, trying to get a better, uh, sight of the house and we'll go from there until I have more personnel.

Officer: Okay.

Officer: D-1 to HQ.

Dispatcher: Go ahead.

Officer: I know you are probably already doing it, but let's, uh, see what kind of registration information we can get from the residents here, and what kind of cars are supposed to be there.

Officer: Roger.

Officer: HQ to D-1, the [redacted]. Uh, give me a minute on the other ones.

Officer: Unit 3.

Dispatcher: There's also a [redacted] registered to that address.

Officer: Okay, those are the two vehicles in the driveway at this time.

Officer: D-1 to A-9.

Officer: Go ahead.

Officer: On the north side of this house where you are, do you have, uh, good setup locations for SRT?

Officer: A-8 to D-1.

Officer: I'm sorry, A-8, go ahead.

Officer: We can't see the house from here, but if we walk around the curve we can see it. [redacted]

Officer: Roger that. There is a gray house to the north of this house. Can you see that?

Officer: If I walk around the curve I can see the gray house.

Officer: I just want to know if anybody is, uh, if it appears anybody is home at that house.

Officer: Uh, if you like I can approach it from the backside and attempt to make contact.

Officer: Look, hold off on the contact, I just want to see if the garage is open or anything like that. We'll use the outside of the residence on the perimeter, [redacted]. Uh, right now we have a closed garage door at this residence. I just want to make sure we have enough bodies before we start making contact.

Officer: Roger.

Officer: Adam 9 to D-1.

Officer: Go ahead, [redacted].

Officer: I would, um, I would take them up on the other side of, uh, Sorghum Mill. I believe that's Hotchkiss behind us. [redacted]

Officer: Roger. Are you still in your same location?

Officer: Roger. I have full visuals of the vehicles, the driveway, and the door leading out of the house to the driveway.

Officer: Roger.

Officer: A-8 to Charlie 3.

Officer: Go ahead.

Officer: Officer [redacted] has your gear down here. Where are you?

Officer: I'm at the rear of the residence. I'm going to need someone to cover my position before I can come over there.

Officer: [redacted]

Officer: A-9 to C-3. Sorry, I got tied up. We have your gear over here. I don't know how you want to make arrangements to get it.

Officer: C-3 to Adam 8.

[Voices in background unintelligible.]

Officer: Delta 5 to Officer [redacted].

Officer: Go ahead.

Officer: C-3's on go ahead.

Officer: C-3, we are on Hotchkiss. We got an eighteen somewhere out, [redacted] it sounds like it's coming from your direction, so just be aware of it. Sounds like he's outside, somebody's outside anyhow.

Officer: Roger, I heard it, too.

Officer: Okay, where is that in location to you? Because we're to the right of where that came from.

Officer: DB unit hold up, you see me.

Officer: Gotcha.

Background: This is what I have so far; we're sitting on Sorghum.

Officer: It came from your right [redacted]. Kind of between that house and the one behind it.

Officer: I stepped on you.

Officer: It came from your right, towards, between that blue house and where you are.

Officer: Okay, is it all set?

Officer: Do not know [redacted]. Looks like we got someone else walking across the street now.

Dispatcher: Police emergency.

[redacted]

Dispatcher: Okay.

[redacted]

Dispatcher: Yes.

Background: C-3 can you copy me?

[redacted]

Dispatcher: Okay.

[redacted]

Dispatcher: Hold on, sir.

[redacted]

Officer: Are you on 911?

[redacted]

Background: Who's this? Who is this? Who is on the phone?

Dispatcher: HQ to all.

Background Dispatcher: This is Officer [redacted], Cheshire Police.

Officer in background: Hey, it's [redacted]. I'm down here [redacted]. All right, get in the house. You two get in the house. Get in the house. I need the 101 here, now, now, [redacted].

Officer: Uh signal fifty-nine, signal fifty-nine, suspects are running into the car. Sir? [redacted].

[redacted]

Dispatcher: Okay.

Officer: [redacted]

Background officers yelling: Now, right here. He's coming. Vehicle is fleeing. [Sirens in background along with yelling.]

Emergency: Ambulance Emergency. What's the address of the emergency?

[Background officers yelling.]

Officer: Yes, I have [redacted].

Background: We got a house fire. We gotta clear the house. [redacted]

Emergency: Okay [redacted].

Officer: Yeah, [redacted].

Background: C-2 stand by for a signal fifty.

Emergency: [redacted] do we know how it was sustained, or no?

[Background noise, sirens, and loudspeaker.]

Dispatcher: I have an officer on scene with him. C-2 Cheshire on the air with a signal fifty, we have a report of a structure fire residence, 300 Sorghum Mill Road. [redacted] C-2 Cheshire on the air with a signal fifty, we have a report of a house fire, structure fire, it will be 300 Sorghum Mill Drive, C-2 on the air, KCD 575.

Officer: Stay indoors, okay? Just stay indoors. All you have to do is stay indoors and lock the doors, okay?

Dispatcher: There's a fire next door most likely.

Emergency: Okay, is that him in the background calling? Okay.

Officer: It's not involving your house [redacted]. We have officers on the scene.

[End of transcript.]

Appendix B:

Cheshire Police Dispatch Log, July 23, 2007

(time, description of activity)

9:21, Initial call comes in on 911; officer speaks with complainant and obtains info on incident. After obtaining info he places the caller on hold.

9:23, Officer picks up 911 call on hold again to obtain further information.

9:24, [redacted]

9:24, [redacted] Caller is told to hold on phone.

9:24, HQ requests [redacted] to call dispatch ASAP.

9:25, [redacted] gives [redacted] a description of incident.

9:25, HQ to all units.

9:26, Initial broadcast of incident at 300 Sorghum Mill Drive.

9:27, Vehicle description is broadcast to units.

9:27, Unit 1 turning onto Higgins from South Main Street.

9:27, [redacted] tells units not to approach the house. [redacted] asks for DB units on the air.

9:28, [redacted]

9:28, Marker plate broadcast to units.

9:29, A-1 asks D-1 if they are en route and says that marked units have been told to stay back from residence. A-1 requests D-1 for drive-by.

9:30, A-4 [redacted] advises he will go to bank to meet complainant.

9:31, A-9 [redacted] to D-1, request to do drive-by of house. D-1 advises patrol units to close both ends of Sorghum Mill Drive.

9:31, [redacted] confirms address with [redacted].

9:31, A. C-3 requests officer doing drive-by to give color and description of house. B. D-1 requests two units to respond to Bank of America. C. A-9 to D-1, Sorghum Mill approaching and will give house info. D. A-4 out at bank. E. A-2 to Unit 2, take position at Sorghum/Nutmeg. F. A-9 gives house info. House faces Hotchkiss Ridge, driveway comes out on Sorghum Mill. [redacted] are parked in driveway. G. C-3 has visual on house. H. C-3 to HQ, have SRT personnel park near car 9.

9:35, A-8 to Unit 3, get my SRT helmet. D-1 is seventy.

9:36, D-1 is doing drive-by.

9:36, HQ to A-9, do you have reg on vehicle in question?

9:36, D-1 to Unit 2, come up to Sorghum/Hotchkiss and A-9, stay where you are.

9:37, D-5 to D-1, after your drive-by can we meet you? I'll meet you at Sorghum Mill and Hotchkiss [AU: OK?] Ridge. A-4 asks for D-1 cell number.

9:38, HQ to A-4. Two-nine [location].

9:39, A-8 to D-2. Correction D-1. He is on a seven.

9:40, Unit 3 to A-8, can I meet you? Come on Mountain Road side. I'm at Sorghum and Burrage Court.

9:40, A-8 asks Unit 3 if he has SRT van.

9:40, C-3 advises A-8 that two SRT officers are on EDJs.

9:41, A-8 asks C-3 if officers are with him, to which he replied no, but just wanted him to be made aware.

9:41, HQ to A-4.

9:42, [redacted] calls back Bank of America to speak with [redacted].

9:42, [redacted] on hold with bank.

9:43, [redacted] on hold with bank.

9:43, [redacted] answers phone at Bank of America and speaks with [redacted] before being called on air by AB.

9:43, AB to HQ, do we have a unit at the bank? Roger A-4.

9:43, AB asks A-4 for any info at this time. A-4 broadcasts [redacted].

9:44, A-4 gives [redacted] an overview of events at bank. [redacted]

9:44, A-1 to D-1, two phone numbers for residence if and when you need them. Also Trooper One [helicopter] is on hold if vehicle leaves residence.

9:44, D-1 advises we need to get perimeter set up before we call. A-1 states he will get Trooper One up in the air.

9:45, [redacted] further describes bank events to [redacted] and requests statement forms.

9:45, D-1, can you give me a second? I have a lot of people talking to me.

9:46, A-8 to D-1. I have three patrol units at Sorghum Mill. D-1 wants two cars at Sorghum/Sorghum and we will move personnel around when we have more personnel here.

9:47, [redacted] are on our way in.

9:48, D-1 to HQ. Request registration info on vehicle for residence.

9:48, [redacted] info given over air.

9:49, [redacted] info given over air.

9:49, D-1 confirms these are the vehicles in the driveway. D-1 to A-9 on the north side of the house. Do you think that is a good setup for SRT [special response team]?

9:51, A-8 to D-1. A-8 recommends setting up command post on Burrage Court. A-9 to D-1 Hotchkiss will allow more coverage.

9:53, A-8 to C-3. I have your gear. [Repeats message.]

9:54, D-5 to [redacted]

9:55, D-5 to C-3. [redacted]

9:55, D-5—[redacted] it's coming from your right.

9:56, D-5 to A-9, do you copy me? A-9—there is activity in the driveway. C-3 signal fifty [redacted] suspects are moving into [redacted]. Car is backing out.

9:56, [redacted] tells [redacted] to send ambulance for [redacted] now.

9:57, Officer [redacted] contacts Campion and advises them that we need an ambulance at [redacted] for a [redacted]. Officer [redacted] also advises them to come in off Mountain Road and that there is a fire also at the scene.

9:57, C-3—Vehicle is fleeing.

9:57, HQ, dispatch the F.D. [fire department]

9:57, D-1 we have a house fire, we have to clear the house.

9:57, F.D. dispatched to 300 Sorghum Mill Drive for house fire/working structure fire.

9:57, 911 call from [redacted].

9:58, Unit 3 to HQ.

9:58, C-1 to C-2. C-1 to C-2.

9:58, Unit 2 to HQ. At intersection of Burrage Court we have [redacted] suspects [redacted].

9:59, A-1 to D-1.

[end of dispatch log]

Appendix C:

Glossary of People Mentioned

Al Adinolfi: Cheshire representative who lived on the same street as the Petits.

Megan Alexander: Seventeen-year-old friend of Hayley Petit. One of the organizers of the Petit Memorial Basketball Tournament. In the fall of 2007 Megan began studies at Syracuse University pursuing a degree in advertising. Daughter of Deb Hereld.

David Atkins: Attorney for the Hartford Courant who, using the Freedom of Information Act, successfully tried to get documents regarding this case unsealed, and protested when Judge Damiani issued a gag order.

Bob Averack: Lived across the street from the Petits.

Pam Averack: Bob's wife, and initiator of the movement to bring the whole Deaconwood neighborhood closer together.

Marilyn Bartoli: One of the organizers of an August 15, 2007 rally in Cheshire calling for increased jail time for repeat offenders. Her child attended the Cheshire Academy.

James M. Bentivegna: Judge who presided over Joshua Komisarjevsky's burglary trial in December 2002.

Ronald Bergamo Jr.: Cheshire homeowner whose house was broken into by Hayes and Komisarjevsky just hours before the Petit murders.

Debbie Biggins: Fifty-year-old witness to Jennifer Hawke-Petit withdrawing $15,000 from the Bank of America in Maplecroft Plaza.

Diane Brady: Friend of the Petits, who made a scarf for Hayley to take to Dartmouth.

Dr. Phil Brewer: Member of the United Methodist congregation, who, after talking to Dr. Petit, came to the conclusion that he was pro-capital punishment.

Reverend John Brinsmade: Pastor of Our Lady of Mercy Church in Plainville, which the elder Petits attend.

Anthony Buglione: Detective. Member of the Connecticut State Police, a twenty-year veteran at the time of the Petit murders, assigned to the Central District Major Crime Squad. His job was to investigate serious and violent crimes, including but not limited to murder. He had received special training in the collection of physical evidence, crime scene processing, and the investigation of such cases.

James Canon Jr.: Detective. Member of the Department of Public Safety, Division of State Police, since February 1997. Was assigned to the Central District Major Crime Squad van in Meriden at the time of the Petit murders. Participated in the search of Komisarjevsky's home.

Bruce Carlson: A board member of Survivors of Homicide, a Connecticut-based organization of families who have lost a loved one to murder.

John Chamberlain: Joshua's grandfather. Married Josh's grandmother Ernestine Stodelle after her first husband Theodore Komisarjevsky died in 1954. Chamberlain was a famous newsman.

Johanna Chapman: Dr. Petit's sister.

Christopher Consorte: Detective. Member of the Connecticut State Police, a ten-year veteran at the time of the Petit murders, assigned to the Central District Major Crime Squad. His job was to investigate serious and violent crimes, including but not limited to murder. He had received special training in the collection of physical evidence, crime scene processing, and the investigation of such cases.

Chris Cote: Police sergeant and member of the SWAT team, who responded to Sorghum Hill Drive on July 23, 2007. His car partially formed the roadblock that stopped the murderers.

Patrick J. Culligan: Defense attorney for Steven Hayes. He was a capital-case expert from the state's chief public defender's office.

Hena Daniels: Reporter for Channel 3 Eyewitness News, interviewed a previous burglary victim of Joshua Komisarjevsky.

Michael Dearington: Prosecutor in the case of triple murder.

Ronald Dearstyne: Prosecutor at Komisarjevsky's burglary trial in December 2002.

Jeremiah Donovan: Defense attorney for Joshua Komisarjevsky. He was a private lawyer appointed by the court.

Christine G. Dunnell: Judge who set the bond for the two suspects at $15 million each.

Barbara Dupre: Coordinated the memorial service for students attending the Cheshire Academy.

Marcy Edington: Friend of Dr. Petit's from medical school. Also one of the organizers of the Precious Petits walk-a-thon team.

Carolyn Hardin Engelhardt: A member of the Petits' church who was the director of the ministry resource center at Yale Divinity School Library.

Tamara Epstein: Lived four houses away from the Petits. She was the creator of the three-bead "Unity" pin to designate Deaconwood residents.

Jamie Erickson: Sophomore at Cheshire High School in 2008, who played in the First Annual Petit Family Memorial Basketball Tournament. Also one of the organizers of the Precious Petits walk-a-thon team.

Kim Ferraiolo: The Petits' next-door neighbor for three years.

John Fixx: Headmaster of Chase Collegiate School, which Michaela Petit attended.

Mrs. A. Burch Tracy Ford: Head of Miss Porter's School, from which Hayley Petit graduated. After the tragedy Mrs. Ford held the student body up on her strong shoulders.

William Gerace: Komisarjevsky's defense attorney at his burglary trial in December 2002.

Laura Gremelsbacker: Public relations director for Cheshire's Lights of Hope.

Auden Grogins: Komisarjevsky's co-counsel during his pre-trial hearings. From Bridgeport, Connecticut.

Matthew Gunsalus: Detective with the Connecticut State Police Central Crime Unit who discovered the location of the red pickup truck.

Jennifer Hawke-Petit: One of the victims. Wife of Dr. William A. Petit, mother of the other two victims. Birthday, September 26, 1958.

Reverend Richard Hawke: Jennifer's father, led six Methodist congregations in western Pennsylvania and was the district superintendent in Pittsburgh before retiring in 1994.

Steven J. Hayes: Forty-four, of Winsted. One of the two suspects in the Petit murders.

Rick Healey: Close friend of the Petit family and Dr. Petit's attorney. Had the job of answering the Petit phone during the long days and weeks following the murders, mostly telling members of the press that the family had no comment.

Sometimes he would add, "The family is devastated over this."

Deb Herald: Friend of the Petits. Attended Hayley's graduation party in June 2006. Mother of Megan Alexander.

Bob Heslin: Organizer of the GE 5K Road Race benefiting the Petit Family Foundation.

David Hick: Cheshire homeowner whose house was broken into by Hayes and Komisarjevsky just hours before the Petit murders.

Justin Ivey: Senior at Cheshire High School in 2008 and one of the organizers of the First Annual Petit Family Memorial Basketball Tournament.

Benedict Komisarjevsky: Joshua's father, an electrical contractor.

Joshua Komisarjevsky: Twenty-six, of Cheshire. One of the alleged perpetrators of the Petit murders.

Jude Komisarjevsky: Joshua's mother. Ben and Jude have been taking care of Joshua's child Jayda since she was a baby. After a bitter court battle, it was decided that the child should stay with her paternal grandparents, who are born-again Christians.

Naomi Komisarjevsky: Joshua's sister.

Theodore Komisarjevsky: Joshua's grandfather, who died in 1954.

Michael P. Lawlor: East Haven Democrat, Connecticut State Representative, and co-chairman of the state legislature's Judiciary Committee.

Wayne Lawrence Jr.: College sophomore pursuing a degree in architecture and one of the organizers of the First Annual Petit Family Memorial Basketball Tournament.

Robert E. Lee: Plainville Town Manager.

Helayne Lightstone: Spokeswoman for the Hospital of Central Connecticut in New Britain where Dr. Petit worked.

Mary Lyons: Bank branch manager who called police after observing Mrs. Petit removing cash from her account, seemingly under duress.

Kevin Mahan: A neighbor of the Petits.

Nancy Manning: A patient of Dr. Petit's. She attended all of the court hearings.

Jay Markella: Police lieutenant with the Cheshire Police Department.

Caroline Mesel: Ex-girlfriend of Komisarjevsky who had recently moved to Arkansas. Komisarjevsky once said he would rob a bank to get her back. At the time she thought he was kidding.

Joy Miller: Classmate of Jennifer Hawke at Greenville High School.

Joan Morin: Patient of Dr. Petit.

Philip Moore: Spokesman for the Cheshire Academy.

Charles I. Motes Jr.: Health director for the town of Southington, filled in as health director for the town of Plainville in Dr. Petit's absence.

Jennifer Norton: Komisarjevsky's girlfriend with whom he had a daughter, Jayda.

Elizabeth Ollero: Harwinton, Connecticut girl who was a friend of Michaela's and created the website forevermichaela.com in her honor.

James Papillo: A Connecticut victim's advocate who proposed the Petit Home Invasion Act, which would reclassify home invasion as a serious felony offense.

Barbara Petit: Dr. Petit's mother.

Glenn Petit: Dr. Petit's brother.

Hayley Petit: Seventeen-year-old victim. Birthday, October 15, 1989.

Michaela Petit: Eleven-year-old victim, born November 17, 1995.

Dr. William A. Petit: A prominent endocrinologist who was present for and survived the fatal attack on his wife and daughters.

Mark and Morgan Raducha: Teenaged siblings who lived across the street from the Petits.

Hope Reinhard: Volunteers coordinator for Cheshire's Lights of Hope.

Cindy Renn: Jennifer Hawke-Petit's sister.

Lisa Riera: Organizer of the January 27, 2008 luminaria in which luminaries were placed along seven miles of Route 10 connecting Southington and Plainville.

Jessica Ryan: Editor of the Cheshire Herald who circulated an online petition calling for stricter laws for repeat offenders.

Walter Ryan: Neighbor of the Petits who, while walking his dog on a Monday morning, witnessed the apprehension of the two murderers.

Steve Selnick: Senior at Cheshire High School and one of the organizers of the First Annual Petit Family Memorial Basketball Tournament.

Jeff Sutherland: Police officer who was stationed at the roadblock on July 23, 2007 and was almost run over by the murderers as they attempted to escape.

Kathryn and Elizabeth Thompson: Two of the organizers of the Precious Petits walk-a-thon team.

Deborah Tom: President of the Plainville Rotary Club.

Charles Turnier: A Burlington, Connecticut man whose home had been burglarized by Joshua Komisarjevsky previous to the Petit murders, while he and his then-pregnant wife were at home.

Tom Ullman: New Haven defense attorney, member of Steven Hayes's defense team.

J. Paul Vance: State police lieutenant who spoke at length during the July 23 press conference.

Jill Veiga: The Petits' next-door neighbor.

Joseph Vitello: Detective. Member of the Cheshire Police Department since August 1985. Participated in the search of Komisarjevsky's home.

Stephen Volpe: The Petits' pastor at Cheshire United Methodist Church.

Don and Jenifer Walsh: Organizers of Cheshire's Lights of Hope.

Loryn Watkinson: Captain's coordinator for Cheshire's Lights of Hope.

Christopher J. Wazorko: a Plainville town councilman.

Tom Wright: Police officer and member of the SWAT team, who responded to Sorghum Hill Drive on July 23, 2007. His car partially formed the roadblock that stopped the murderers.

Steve Zarmsky: Organizer of the Petit Family Foundation Golf Tournament.

Bibliography

Altimari, Dave, and Colin Poitras. "Cheshire Dispatch Log Released: Nearly 5 Minutes Elapsed Between 911 Call and Police Broadcast." Courant.com, January 22, 2008. Website of the *Hartford Courant*.

Begnal, Martin. "Cheshire neighborhood unites after tragedy." Rep-am.com, September 23, 2007. Website of the *Republican-American*.

Bloom, Lary. "As School Mourns Its Own, Virtues Come to Light," Nytimes.com, March 9, 2008.

"Censored Police Log Details Cheshire Response: Officers Told to Hold Back During Home Invasion." Wfsb.com, January 22, 2008.

"Cheshire Home Invasion Suspects Due in Court." Nbc30.com, March 11, 2008.

"Cheshire Homicides: Police response time was nearly 5 minutes after 911 call." Myrecordjournal.com, January 23, 2008.

"Cheshire Murder Suspects Appear in Court: Why did petty criminals turn to murder?" Cnn.com, transcript of interview that aired August 7, 2007.

"Cheshire Murder Suspects' Bail Set At $15 Million." Wcbstv.com, July 24, 2007.

"Cheshire Pays Tribute to Petits: Community Gathers to Support Survivor." Thebostonchannel.com, September 20, 2007.

Christoffersen, John. "Conn. Home Invasion Suspects in Court: 2 Men Accused of Burglarizing Conn. Home, Killing 3 Make Brief, Tense Court Appearance." ABCNews.com, August 8, 2007.

—————————. "Suspect in Conn. Home invasion discussed crime with girlfriend." Boston.com, October 30, 2007.

Collins, Dave. "Officials labeled suspect a risk to society before home invasion." The *Providence Journal*, April 3, 2008.

Cowan, Allison Leigh. "Death Penalty Tests a Church as It Mourns." Nytimes.com, October 28, 2007.

—————————. "Rell Urges Strengthening Connecticut Justice System." Nytimes.com, January 9, 2008.

—————————. "Warrants Give Details of Killings of 3 in July." Nytimes.com, October 24, 2007.

Cowan, Allison Leigh, and Stacey Stowe. "Suspects Face Jeers and Victims' Family in New Haven." Nytimes.com, August 8, 2007.

—————————. "Uncle of Suspect in Cheshire Home Invasion Speaks." Nytimes.com, July 26, 2007.

"Criminal Psychologist Discusses Cheshire Homicides." Thebostonchannel.com, July 25, 2007.

"Donations Pour In to Remember Home Invasion Victims." Wnbc.com, July 31, 2007.

"'Dunk It' Tourney Honors Petits: Money Raised to Benefit Multiple Sclerosis Research." Wfsb.com, March 15, 2008.

"Family Deaths Prompt Order to Increase Parole Checks." Nytimes.com, August 1, 2007.

Fernandez, Manny. "Petit Family's Prominence Was Founded in Good Will." Nytimes.com, July 25, 2007.

—————————. "Tears and Reminiscences for Three Murder Victims." *New York Times*, July 29, 2007.

Fernandez, Manny, and Alison Leigh Cowan. "When Horror Came to a Connecticut Family." Nytimes.com, August 7, 2007

"Find Out How to Protect Your Home From an Invasion." Abcnews.com, July 25, 2007.

"Friends Take Up Cause of 'Precious Petits': Connecticut Community Comes Together to Honor Causes Important to Petit Family." Abcnews.com, September 26, 2007.

Glidden, Rob. "Community to shine in honor of Petit family." The Step Saver/ *The Observer,* January 17, 2008, p. 4.

"Gun Sales Rise After Cheshire Home Invasion: Security Company Says Phones Ringing Off Hook." The bostonchannel. com, July 26, 2007.

Haigh, Susan. "Thousands Mourn Doctor's Slain Family." Associated Press dispatch, July 28, 2007.

Haigh, Susan, and Dave Collins. "State says suspects in Cheshire murders showed no violent signs." Boston.com, July 25, 2007.

"Home invasion suspect appears in court." Wtnh.com, March 31, 2008.

"Home Invasion Suspects Face Murder Charges." Cbsnews .com, July 27, 2007.

"Horror in the Night." *People Magazine.* August 2, 2007.

Hughes, Paul. "Cheshire victims' family pushes for 3 strikes law." Rep-am.com, March 13, 2008.

————. "State House sends crime bill to Rell." Rep-am.com, April 26, 2008.

"Hundreds Expected to Attend Petit Memorial: Mourners to Gather at Cheshire Football Field." Thebostonchannel.com, September 19, 2007.

Hutchison, Leslie. "Cheshire Academy plans private memorial." Myrecordjournal.com, August 28, 2007.

————. "Cheshire Homicides: Strong defense promised in triple homicide case." Myrecordjournal.com, August 2, 2007.

—————. "Cheshire lights signal hope and healing for Petit and town." Myrecordjournal.com, January 7, 2007.

—————. "Luminaria will benefit Petit children's Miracle Memorial." Myrecordjournal.com, September 30, 2007.

—————. "Motes was quick to pinch-hit for Petit in Plainville." Myrecordjournal.com, January 24, 2008.

—————. "Witness saw Hawke-Petit in bank on fatal day." Myrecordjournal.com, July 28, 2007.

"Introducing evil to the debate." Rep-am.com, April 2, 2008.

"Judiciary Committee Hears from Dr. Petit: Committee Considering Changes to Parole System." Wfsb.com, November 27, 2007.

Kaplan, Thomas. "New Haven: Murder Suspects Plead Not Guilty." Nytimes.com, November 2, 2007.

Mancini, Marissa. "To Wal-Mart, or Not to Wal-Mart?" Central Connecticut State University Recorder, February 6, 2008.

Mayko, Michael P. "Legislature OKs tougher break-in bill." Ctpost.com, January 23, 2008.

Michel, Robin Lee. "Plainville memorial draws thousands." Myrecordjournal.com, July 31, 2007.

Michels, Scott. "Police Nearby During Deadly Home Invasion: Police Ordered Not to Approach Home Where 3 Killed While Perimeter Set Up." Abcnews.com, January 24, 2008.

Murphy, Dennis. "Desperate Hours." Msnbc.com, September 10, 2007.

O'Donnell, Marianne. "Knocking on Doors in Cheshire, Conn." Msnbc.com, September 10, 2007.

"Parole Ban Protested Outside Prison: Released Prisoner Discusses Prison Conditions." Wfsb.com, November 26, 2007.

"Parole Discussed at Public Hearing: Changes Called for After Cheshire Home Invasion." Wfsb.com, November 26, 2007.

"Past Komisarjevsky Victim Speaks Out: Man Says Cheshire Suspect Burglarized His Home." Wfsb.com, posted July 26, 2007, accessed February 29, 2008.

Pazniokas, Mark. "Three Strikes Law Backed: Petit Relative Addresses Panel." Courant.com, March 13, 2008.

"Petit Family Holds Private Funeral: Hospital Releases Dr. William Petit Jr." Wfsb.com, July 27, 2007.

Phaneuf, Keith M. "Would proposals have stopped Cheshire home invaders?" *Journal Inquirer*, January 9, 2008.

Powell, Chris. "State Commentary—Sex offender hysteria produces no protection for public." *The Stamford Times*, March 21, 2008.

Ramiunni, Kate. "Speakers offer tips in case of home invasion." Ctpost.com, February 27, 2008.

Ryan, Jessica. "A Change is Needed." *The Cheshire Herald*, April 3, 2008.

Salerno, Carolee. "Teens organize basketball tournament to honor Petit family." Wtnh.com, March 15, 2008.

"School Head Runs 'Miles for Michaela': John Carpenter Will Run the NYC Marathon in Honor of Slain Student Michaela Petit." Abcnews.com, November 5, 2007.

"Security firm will donate to Petits' cause." Myrecordjournal.com, August 19, 2007.

Sheyner, Gennady. "Call to faith, action over evil: Doctor speaks at memorial service for his family." Rep-am.com, July 29, 2007.

Stowe, Stacey. "Death Penalty Bid in 3 Killings Draws Critics." Nytimes.com, July 28, 2007.

Strillacci, Elisabeth. "Cheshire Homicides: Judge imposes gag order in Cheshire case." Myrecordjournal.com, November 6, 2007.

—————. "Evidence collection ongoing in Cheshire." Myrecordjournal.com, August 1, 2007.

Stuart, Christine. "Neighbors of Home Invasion Victims Demand Stricter Repeat-Offender Laws." Nytimes.com, August 16, 2007.

"Three-Strikes Bill Loses in Committee: Some Vow to Press for Measure for Persistent Violent Offenders." Courant.com, March 20, 2008.

Tuhus, Melinda. "Walker Questions Post-Petit Proposals." *New Haven Independent*, November 28, 2007.

Turmelle, Luther, and Phil Helsel. "Alleged killers followed Petits home from market." Newbritainherald.com, July 26, 2007.

Van Zandt, Clint. "A history of violence: The Petit family were victims of a home invasion and brutal murder. Will sociopath behavior ever be understood?" Msnbc.msn.com, July 25, 2007.

Velardi, Chris. "Website dedicated to Petit girl gets national attention." Wtnh.com, February 8, 2008.

Wittenberg, Adam. "Petit case may be in court for years." Myrecordjournal.com, April 13, 2008.

Wolff, Elizabeth, and Ginger Adams Otis. "Vicious Fiends Stalked Victims from Food Store." Nypost.com, July 29, 2007.

Where to Send Donations

Cheshire's Lights of Hope
P.O. Box 553
Cheshire CT 06410

The GE 5K Road Race Benefiting the Petit Family
Foundation
P.O. Box 310
Plainville, CT 06062-0310

Hayley's Hope or Michaela's Miracle
National Multiple Sclerosis Society
Greater CT Chapter
659 Tower Avenue, 1st Floor
Hartford, CT 06112
www.ctfightsms.org

Hayley Petit Scholarship
Miss Porter's School
60 Main Street
Farmington, CT 06032

Jennifer Hawke-Petit Scholarship
Cheshire Academy
10 Main Street
Cheshire, CT 06410

Miles for Michaela
Make checks payable to: Chase Collegiate School for
the Michaela Petit Scholarship Fund
565 Chase Parkway
Waterbury CT 06708
milesformichaela.org

The Petit Family Foundation
P.O. Box 310
Plainville, CT 06062-0310

The Petit Family Foundation Golf Tournament
P.O. Box 310
Plainville, CT 06062-0310

Precious Petit Foundation
c/o Cheshire United Methodist Church
205 Academy Road
Cheshire CT 06410

Shining Peace Upon the Petits
P.O. Box 634
Plantsville, CT 06479
www.shiningpeace.org

To sponsor a team in the Annual Petit Family Memorial
Basketball Game please visit petitmemorialbball.com.

Index

A

Alexander, Megan, 100–101, 184–85, 186–88
Averack, Bob, 45

B

Bank of America, 11–12
Bergamo, Ronald, Jr., 44
Biggins, Deborah, 13, 15, 35–36
Board of Pardons and Parole, 118–19, 165
burglary, 9, 43–45, 51

C

Caligiuri, Sam, 39
candlelight vigil, 107–9
cell phones, 31
Chapman, Johanna, 37
Chase Collegiate School, 194–97
Cheshire, CT, xiii, 4–5
  anger at justice system and, 134–37
  Cheshire's Lights of Hope, 169–72
  community support, 32, 33
  crisis response and, 38
  curiosity seekers, 32
  Deaconwood neighborhood, 140–42
  effect on community, 45, 48, 85–90, 138–39
  March Madness, 184–88
  memorial service, 149–51
Cheshire Academy, 197–98
Cheshire's Lights of Hope, 169–72
Chief Medical Examiner, 30
Connelly, John A., 85

Cornwall Avenue, 14
criminals, xii–xiii
Cruess, Michael, 26, 47
Culligan, Patrick J.
  initial court appearance and, 126
  media coverage and, 130

D

Dearing, Michael, 130
Dearington, Michael, 39–40, 84
death penalty
  announcement of pursuit of, 84
  criteria for, 85
  defense attorney statements, 84
  United Methodist Church and, 143–48
donations, 109–12
Donovan, Jeremiah
  initial court appearance and, 127
  media coverage and, 129–30
Dunnell, Christina G., 37

F

Farmington Linear Park Bike Route, 15
Farr, Robert, 39
Ferraiolo, Kim, 33
fire, 19, 21–22, 27–28
First Annual Petit Family Foundation Golf Tournament, 152–53

G

Garnett, Brian, 40
getaway attempt, 19–20
Greater Connecticut Chapter of the National Multiple Sclerosis Society, 109–10, 184–86

H

Haas, Genevieve, 34
Harry Potter, 8
Hawke, Richard
  candlelight vigil, 107
  on scene of crime, 32
Hawke-Petit, Jennifer
  burns on, 27
  Cheshire Academy and, 197–98
  death of, 18, 19
  description of, 2
  family of, 32
  funeral services for, 91–92, 93,
    95–96, 97
  Greenville, PA memorial, 103–4
  multiple sclerosis and, 35–36,
    109–10
  return home from Stop & Shop,
    3
  trip to bank, 11–15
Hayes, Steven
  anger at, 40, 125
  burglaries by, 44–45
  charges against, 83–84
  criminal activity, 79–81
  early criminal sentences, 79–80
  family background of, 79
  family statements, 46
  halfway house and, 77–78
  parole status, 37, 38–39, 116
  profile of, 42
  vehicle of, 23
Hick, David, 44–45
home, description of, 5–6, 203

I

In Cold Blood, 40–41
investigation
  arson, 27–28
  autopsies, 30
  Komisarjevsky home, 28–30

press conference and, 24–26
  processing of scene, 27
  search warrants, 23, 30–32
  suspect vehicles, 22–23

J

justice system
  argument for reforms, 46
  call for stricter laws, 134–37
  criticism by William A. Petit, Sr.,
    130–31
  law modifications, 161–62,
    163–67, 183
  Leslie Williams and, 175–76
  monitoring criminals, 137–38
  parole board, 165
  public hearings regarding,
    162–63
  sex offenders and, 181–82
  William Petit letter and, 160–61

K

Komisarjevsky, Christopher, 46
Komisarjevsky, Joshua
  anger at, 40, 125
  burglaries by, 43–45, 46–47, 51,
    52, 76
  Caroline Mesel and, 153–57
  charges against, 83–84
  community recollections of,
    104–6
  court proceedings and, 52–76
  description of, 78
  early criminal activities, 50–51
  family background of, 49–50
  family statements, 46
  parole status, 37, 38–39, 116
  profile of, 42
  release from halfway house,
    78–79
  release to halfway house, 76–77

sexual issues, 76
vehicle of, 22–23
Komisarjevsky, Jude, 28–30

L
Lightstone, Helayne, 33–34
Lyons, Mary, 13–14, 15

M
Manning, Nancy, 33
Maplecroft Shopping Plaza, 1–2, 3
Markella, Jay, 48
media
   coverage of story and, 100–101
   criminal profiles, 40–42, 132–33
   criticism of government
      response, 122–23
   effects of crime on, 33
   families of criminals, 45–47
   gag order and, 157–59, 178
   initial statement by family, 35
   Petit family statement, 82, 102–3
   Petit neighbors and, 138
   press conference, 24–27
   rumors and, 47–48
   trial coverage and, 129–30
Mesel, Caroline, 153–57
Miss Porter's School, 189–94
Monahan, James, 42
Morin, Joan, 33
Mountain Road, 15

N
911 transcript, 167–68, 204–17

O
Ollero, Elizabeth, 199–202

P
Petit, Glenn, 45
Petit, Hayley
   announcement of death, 34
   burns on, 27
   candlelight vigil, 109
   death of, 19
   description of, 6–8
   funeral services for, 92, 93,
      95–96, 97–98
   Miss Porter's School and, 189–94
Petit, Johanna, 178–79
Petit, Michaela
   burns on, 27
   candlelight vigil, 109
   Chase Collegiate School, 194–97
   cooking and, 6
   death of, 19
   description of, 2
   Elizabeth Ollero and, 199–202
   flower fundraiser and, 159
   funeral services for, 92–93, 95–96,
      98–99
Petit, William A., Jr.
   candlelight vigil, 107–9
   Cheshire memorial service and,
      150–51
   crime aftermath, 203
   criticism of, 123–24
   description of, 33, 34
   escape of, 18, 19
   family background of, 96
   Glenn Petit on, 45
   initial attack on, 9
   letter regarding justice system,
      160–61
   occupation of, 6, 36–37
   professional duties, 36
   speech at funeral services,
      96–100
Petit, William A., Sr., 130–31
Petit Family Foundation, 111–12,
   152–53, 159, 188
Pidgeon, Robert, 40

Plainville, CT, 37–38, 172–74
police
    aid to William Petit, 18–19
    arrival at bank, 15
    arrival at home, 16
    capture of criminals, 20–21
    criticsm of, 120–21
    dispatch log, 218–21
    evidence collection and, 117–18
    getaway attempt and, 19–20
    investigation of scene, 22, 27, 28
    Komisarjevsky home and,
        28–30, 113
    mobilization on scene, 17
    911 transcript, 167–68, 204–17
    press conference omissions, 26
    report of crime and, 13–14
    search warrants, 23, 30–32,
        93–95

Q
Quarry Village, 10–11

R
Raducha, Mark, 28
Raducha, Morgan, 28
Rising, Ronald A., 33

S
search warrants
    for cell phones, 115–16
    for clothing, 114
    for computer, 30
    for persons, 31–32
    for phone records, 114–15
    public and, 151–52
    for vehicles, 93–95
Shining Peace Upon the Petits,
    172–74
Sorghum Mill Drive, 3, 5

stalking of victims, 3–4
Super Stop & Shop, 2

T
Tom, Deborah, 38
trial
    anger at defendants, 125–26
    court hearing before, 148
    expected time frame for, 131–32
    Hayes' initial appearance, 126–27
    Komisarjevsky's initial appear-
        ance, 127–28
    security for, 125–26, 128
Turnier, Charles, 43–44

U
United Methodist Church, 143–48

V
Van Zandt, Cliff, 40–42
Vance, J. Paul, 24–26
Veiga, Jill, 48
Volpe, Stephen, 34–35

W
Wazorko, Christopher J., 38
Welsh, Mary Ellen, 175–76
Williams, Leslie, 175–76

About the Author

Michael Benson is the author or co-author of fifty books, including the true-crime books *Betrayal in Blood*, *Lethal Embrace*, and *Hooked Up for Murder*. He's also written *Inside Secret Societies*, *Who's Who in the JFK Assassination* (both Citadel), and *Complete Idiot's Guides to NASA*, *National Security*, *The CIA*, *Submarines*, and *Modern China* (all from Penguin). Other works include biographies of Ronald Reagan, Bill Clinton, and William Howard Taft. Originally from Rochester, New York, he is a graduate of Hofstra University.